Stephe

CITY SUGAR

Edited by Tim Bezant

THE HEREFORD PLAYS

HEINEMANN · METHUEN

HEREFORD PLAYS

Heinemann Educational Books Ltd
Halley Court, Jordan Hill, Oxford OX2 8EJ
OXFORD LONDON EDINBURGH
MELBOURNE SYDNEY AUCKLAND
IBADAN NAIROBI GABORONE HARARE
KINGSTON PORTSMOUTH NH (USA)
SINGAPORE MADRID

First published in Methuen New Theatrescripts in 1976.
First published in revised edition as Methuen Modern Play 1978.
First published in this edition by Heinemann/Methuen 1989.
Copyright © 1976, 1978 by Stephen Poliakoff.
Introduction and notes copyright © 1989 by Tim Bezant
Music and lyrics of *Yellow Blues* and *I Can Give You
Love* copyright © 1976 by Hugh Thomas

ISBN: 0 435 22581 2

Typeset by
Taurus Graphics, Abingdon, Oxfordshire
Printed in Great Britain by
Richard Clay Ltd, Bungay, Suffolk

Contents

Introduction   iv
  Stephen Poliakoff   iv
  City Sugar   v
  Further Reading and References   vii

CITY SUGAR   1

Activities and Explorations   99
  Keeping Track   99
  Explorations   104
    Characters   104
    Themes   107
    In Performance   108
    Criticism   108

Appendix
  Plays and Films of Stephen Poliakoff   110

INTRODUCTION

Stephen Poliakoff

Stephen Poliakoff was born in 1952 to a Russian father and an English mother. His family had a theatrical background: his mother had been an actress, while his maternal grandmother had two plays presented in London's West End.

He started writing plays while attending Westminster School: his first play, *Granny*, was presented there in 1969. He continued to write while at Cambridge University, where he read History. More important, however, was the first professional production of one of his plays, *Day With My Sister*, in Edinburgh in 1971. The favourable reception this received encouraged him to leave university before taking his degree to take up writing full-time. Over the seven years between 1972 and 1979 Poliakoff's work was prolific, with many of his early plays being produced at small 'fringe' theatres in London.

It was at one of these fringe theatres, The Bush (located above a pub in London's Shepherd's Bush), that *City Sugar* was first produced in 1975 when Poliakoff was twenty-three. Its success led to its transferring to the Comedy Theatre in London's West End (where Adam Faith took the leading role). It established Poliakoff as a new and important writer to whom attention should be paid. This was confirmed by his winning the London Evening Standard Drama Award for the Most Promising Playwright of 1976 and by his being invited to become Writer-in-Residence at the then newly-opened National Theatre for 1976–77.

It was at the National Theatre that his next play, *Strawberry Fields*, was presented in 1977. Subsequent plays included *The Summer Party*, *American Days* and *Favourite Nights*, all presented by more established theatre companies than had presented his earlier work. In 1984 the Royal Shakespeare Company presented *Breaking the*

Silence, a play based on the experiences of his grandfather in pre-Revolutionary Russia. His most recent stage play is *Coming in to Land*, which was presented at the National Theatre in 1986.

With his success in the theatre came the opportunity to write for television: *Stronger than the Sun*, set in the nuclear power industry, was broadcast by the BBC in 1978, to be followed in 1980 by *Caught on a Train*, which won the British Academy of Film and Television Arts Best Single Television Play award. This in turn led to Poliakoff writing film screenplays, for the film *Runners* (about a father's search for his runaway daughter on the streets of London) and for *Hidden City*, which was Poliakoff's first film as a director.

Hence Poliakoff has broadened the range and style of his beginnings, while remaining a forceful and effective writer. You will find a full list of his work to date in the appendix on page 110.

City Sugar

City Sugar was written and first presented in 1975. The play attracted attention because of its setting, its characters and their interaction with the central character, the disc-jockey Leonard Brazil.

Setting and Period
Most of the play takes place in the studio of Leicester Sound, a fictional local commercial radio station. When the play was written, the Independent Local Radio network was still new and developing. The first two stations (LBC and Capital in London) had come on air only two years before in 1973, and by the end of 1975 only fifteen stations were operating (by the end of 1988 there were 46). As these stations broke the monopoly on radio broadcasting previously held by the BBC they changed the nature and style of radio broadcasting, having to attract listeners to ensure the necessary advertising revenue. The play presents a fictional, extreme, darkly comic yet serious example of the

lengths to which stations might soon be prepared to go in order to captivate and keep listeners.

At the end of Act One Leonard Brazil says 'this is nineteen hundred and seventy eight': hence, at the time of writing, Poliakoff was setting the play in the not-too-distant future. Many of the features of this radio station are recognisable today: it may be that the warnings the play sounds about the type of broadcasting it depicts are even more pertinent today.

In Performance

For a successful presentation of the play, three sets would be required: a detailed setting for the Leicester Sound studio, and possibly lesser settings to represent the supermarket where Nicola Davies works and her bedroom. In performance it is necessary too for the action to move from one setting to the next quickly and smoothly to maintain the continuity of the play: this would obviously place constraints on the size and layouts of the different sets. It is worth trying to visualise how this problem might be solved as a means of adding detail to a reading of the play.

Unless the play is presented as a period piece – which would kill it stone dead – the records played that are intended to be hits at the time of the play would need to be updated, as might other references to successful groups or the news. The records that are intended to be golden oldies should not, however, be updated or the intended effect would be lost.

Reading the Play

All plays are written to be performed or, at the very least, read aloud. In the case of *City Sugar* this is doubly true. Much of the play takes place 'on air' and it is vital to hear Leonard Brazil in action, as his fictional audience would hear him. It is also important to read the play aloud in order to hear and appreciate the interaction of the various sets of characters, as well as to appreciate what is left unsaid and unwritten.

Because the play is principally constructed of scenes for

between two to four characters, it obviously lends itself well to reading aloud in groups of this size. Read aloud first of all to understand the action and the relationships; then explore and experiment with the text to discover more depth and understanding of the characters and their changing relationships.

Following the play text you will find two series of questions. Those in the section headed **Keeping Track** are intended to help in understanding the action as it develops and can be used while reading the play for the first time. Under the heading **Explorations** are more detailed and demanding questions organised according to Character, Theme, Performance and Criticism. The questions in the latter section may lead into coursework assignments. All the questions are designed to stimulate knowledge, understanding and, hopefully, enjoyment of the play.

Tim Bezant

Further Reading and References

The New British Drama	Oleg Kerensky (Hamish Hamilton, 1977)
British Theatre Since 1955	Ronald Hayman (Cambridge University Press, 1979)
Contemporary English Drama	Ed. C. W. E. Bigsby (Edward Arnold, 1981)
A Short Guide to Modern British Drama	John Russell Brown (Heinemann Educational Books, 1982)
Contemporary Dramatists	Ed. D. L. Kirkpatrick (St James's Press, 1988)

City Sugar was first staged at the Bush Theatre, Shepherd's Bush, London on 9 October 1975, with the following cast:

LEONARD BRAZIL	John Shrapnel
REX	Leon Vitali
NICOLA DAVIES	Lynne Miller
SUSAN	Natasha Pyne
BIG JOHN	James Beattie
JANE	Hilary Gasson

Directed by Hugh Thomas

The play, in the revised version printed here, was subsequently presented by Michael White at the Comedy Theatre, London on 4 March 1976, with the following cast:

LEONARD BRAZIL	Adam Faith
REX	James Aubrey
NICOLA DAVIES	Lynne Miller
SUSAN	Natasha Pyne
BIG JOHN	Alan Hay
JANE	Hilary Gasson
MICK	Michael Tarn

Directed by Hugh Thomas

The action takes place in a sound studio of Leicester Sound, a local commercial radio station; in the Leicester branch of British Home Stores or Liptons (frozen foods counter); and in Nicola's bedroom in Leicester.

The time is the present.

CITY SUGAR

Characters

LEONARD: in his middle to late thirties, extremely polished appearance, but dresses stylishly rather than ultra-fashionably, considerable natural charm, even when being aggressive.

REX: twenty-one years old, a mixture of eager awkwardness and cockiness. He has a likeable naive manner.

NICOLA: sixteen years old. Totally flat voice, but a very determined manner underneath the quiet, completely blank exterior.

SUSAN: is also sixteen, extremely volatile, attractive manner, with a lot of highly charged violence insider her.

BIG JOHN: small shiny man, in his late fifties, totally accepting manner; tidy, neat, completely dedicated to his job.

JANE: sixteen years old, quite a sharp competitive manner, but also nervous, and completely overcome by her surroundings.

MICK: shy seventeen-year-old, overjoyed to be working where he is.

Author's Note

It is important that Leonard's style as a disc-jockey is not too transatlantic, but his own special blend of relaxed charm, sudden fluent bursts of energy, and barbed comment. He is totally in control of his medium, and his actions round his desk and controls should suggest a master disc-jockey. The tension inside him which explodes later in the play should build up gradually, both on and off the microphone – his considerable charm in the first scene, both to his audience and to Rex, getting progressively more and more sour, until eventually it becomes savage.

However, he never allows himself to over-step the mark *completely* when he is on the air, even in his huge speech at the end of the first act.

ACT ONE

Scene One

The studio, LEONARD BRAZIL *is sitting at the record desk.* REX *is in the engineer's box. A pop record fades over a blackout.*

LEONARD (*into the mike*): From 1968, there, Amen Corner, featuring the unmistakable soprano of Mr Andre Fairweather-Low, and 'If Paradise Was Half As Nice'. Welcome back to the LB show . . . LB – the two most important initials in the country. LB on five hundred and fifty waves – that's a lot of water. (*Loud.*) *Five hundred and fifty* medium waves! (*Smiles.*) Sorry. 'You can do better than that, Brazil.' 'Yes Boss.' In a few minutes we have something for you, something special. (*Beginning to open letters on the turn-table desk.*) I want to say hello to those I met in North Street yesterday; people out in their gardens with *Green* fingers, very definitely, and green feet too, so I'm told. And one even with green hair. No, it was very nice meeting you. they have lovely gardens up there, don't they, lovely houses! (*In his more normal voice.*) I have a few letters in front of me – I've been struggling to open. I have one from Mrs Lee, Mrs D. Lee, saying that did I know there was now a topless restaurant in this fine city of ours, and its name is the Aubergine – how's that for a free commercial, you guys over there in the Aubergine – and Mrs Lee wonders, what do I think about it? I think – it's a very classy name, '*The Aubergine*', perhaps in French it is something more than just a vegetable. I wonder, since we're being blue – or blue*ish*, perhaps we could ask – would any of the ladies like to see bottomless waiters approaching you

1

with your curry? Rex is suggesting a lot of rude vegetable jokes about what that restaurant would be called, which I will ignore. Enough of this smut . . . I went to the cinema yesterday, saw the very excellent *Death Wish*, a lot of rape and gore and blood and guts, for those of you that like your toast buttered that way – me, I prefer the lovely, the scintillating, the mind-expanding Lynsey De Paul. (*Over the beginning of the record, which he has switched on.*) Nobody need fear – Lynsey De Paul is here . . .

He turns a switch, after a few bars so that the music now plays silently while the record goes round; he drops his biro onto the desk. Pause.

LEONARD: That was execrable. (*He flicks the intercom to speak to* REX *in the box.*) That was a real stinker. A loosener – and a very loose loosener at that. (*Pause. He continues to the intercom.*) Come in here . . . It's the sleepy time for them at the moment, all gorged after Sunday lunch, lying in heaps round the room . . . they won't want to be stirred. (*Pause. Louder into the intercom.*) Get yourself in here, right now!

REX *enters behind him.*

REX: I'm here.

LEONARD: That's better.

REX: I've brought a drink.

LEONARD: How kind . . . (*Slight smile.*) Trying to placate me are you? . . . What is it?

REX: Lime juice; it's a free sample of one of the commercials we're carrying this week. I thought you'd like to try it.

LEONARD: It looks like a congealed shampoo. (*He puts it to one side. Suddenly staring at* REX; *loud.*) Now, why haven't you filled these up?

REX: I was going to.

LEONARD: Going to! Everybody keeps on telling me how efficient you are, how fortunate I am to have you. I have yet to notice. Go and do these now. (*Hands him sheets of record titles to be filled in.*) I warn you, it's a particularly grisly lot. (*Smiles.*) I seem to have played pap for an entire week – might as well have stuck the stylus into cotton wool. (REX *moves slightly.*) And why hasn't my mail been checked . . .

REX (*embarrassed*): Sorry, I . . .

LEONARD (*holding up letter*): I've been asked to open another municipal pleasure pond – which is completely out of the question of course.

REX: Why?

LEONARD (*rifling through his other letters*): The last time – the one and only time I had to baptise a pond – it was in front of councillors and crowds, and all the rest . . . and I had to launch it – with a champagne bottle, containing – (*Suddenly looking up.*) – and this is completely and utterly true – frog's spawn. A bottleful. I wasn't allowed to smash it against the side of course, I had to solemnly pour it out, and of course the bloody stuff got stuck and I had to stand there shaking it, and banging the bottom, like a ketchup bottle, until of course I got it all over myself. (*Looks up.*) What I really hate is somebody that doesn't believe a good true story. (*Loud.*) Get on with it! (REX *moves slightly. Loud.*) What's more, I've never seen a single person even *near* that pond – thousands of pounds spent on a small windswept hole in completely the wrong place.

REX: I . . . By the way – I've left an item there – (*He*

indicates the desk.) – you might like.

LEONARD: You have, have you. Worse and worse, Rex . . . You're having a good day, aren't you? (*Smiles*.) I don't like suggestions very much, you should know that by now.

REX: Yeah but I thought – you could . . . I wanted . . .

LEONARD: No! (*He turns suddenly to the mike, turns on the record over the monitor speakers, fades it down*.) That was Miss De Paul. I'm now struggling with another letter on pink paper – it's from Mrs Joan Parsons saying 'Dear Leonard, Is it true or false that you were a teacher in another life?' Well, now, I don't know about another life, Joan, but I was in this one, yes. I trained as a teacher as it happens, before I slipped into the record business, and when all that went up in a puff of smoke, I slipped back into the classroom, until of course I heard the call of Leicester Sound. I thought that everybody knew that, Joan. (*Smiles*.) A joke. And a note here from a theatre group calling itself the Gracious Players, saying, could I give a free plug to their production of the late Dame Agatha Christie's *Towards Zero* on Saturday at the Town Hall, Hinkley, which seats one thousand five hundred people. No wonder they wanted their free mention. And I'm now being handed by the ever-dependable Rex, a piece of paper on which is written 'DON'T FORGET'. And if you don't know what that means, I do, and I'll tell you in a moment, for we have a real thriller coming up; but to change the subject – (*Putting on a record*.) – I have lost some weight. In fact I've lost so much weight, I'm floating out of my seat, floating round the studio. They've had to weigh down my trousers with Encyclopaedia Britannicas! (*Normal*.) While our friend Rex is gaining all the time, I'm afraid, he's approaching sixteen stone now, a hunky piece of flesh, can hardly fit into his box. Enough of this gibberish. 'DON'T FORGET' means competition time. We have a stunner for you in a moment . . . till then, let's flash back into the dim distant past of last week. (*He switches on a record; 'It's Gonna Sell A Million'; and turns the sound off after a couple of bars.*) That was better – that was very slightly better.

    He gets up, walks.

REX (*entering*): Why do you keep on doing this?

LEONARD: Doing what?

REX: You know . . .

LEONARD: Putting weight on you, you mean – making you an obese lump. It's my rather dismal little joke.

REX: I thought . . . you were the one for the truth over the air.

LEONARD: I allow myself this one slight distortion.

REX: But people will discover, won't they?

LEONARD: No they won't, nobody's ever going to publish a picture of you, are they?

REX: Yes. (*Pause.*) The local press might.

LEONARD (*smiling*): Not with shares in this station they won't. In fact a total wall of silence could be preserved about your real size for evermore. In fact if I wanted I could pump you up steadily to twenty-five stone and then burst you. (*Pause.*) Sorry. (*Smiles.*) Don't worry, I do it to everyone that works for me.

REX: So I've heard.

LEONARD: So there's no need to look injured. You're not, yet.

    REX *moves to go.*

REX (*slight smile*): By the way, I've got Capital on the line.

5

LEONARD (*without looking up*): You'll have to be more convincing than that. Been listening to jabber and gossip, have you?

REX: I suppose so, yes.

LEONARD: Well, don't.

REX (*watching him*): Everybody knows anyway. Are they going to make an offer them?

LEONARD: It's just possible. Everything's possible. I shouldn't bank on it.

REX: For the afternoon show . . . (*Smiles.*) they'll be sending spies up here. They'll be sitting in pubs with transistors and earplugs, listening away. You'll have to give them the whole works.

LEONARD (*looking up*): Will I . . . Get it ready.

REX: It is ready.

LEONARD (*totally matter-of-fact*): You can have a moment longer than usual, because I'm in a generous mood.

REX: Thanks . . . I –

LEONARD (*cutting him off, swinging round to the mike and switching on the monitor speakers, fading down the end of the record*): And now, a special competition. You heard me – a mind-tingling competition. And by my side is the ever-dependable Rex, sweating slightly, what have we got as a prize, Rex?

REX (*nervous, standing by the mike and speaking into it, putting on an almost BBC voice*): We have *their* latest LP – the Yellow Jack's latest?

LEONARD (*brash voice*): Tell us the title, Rex – *please* tell us the title.

REX: 'High Up There'.

LEONARD: That's a fine title – is it a fine record?

REX: It's very exciting Leonard, it really is . . .

LEONARD (*to the listeners*): And you can have it a whole two

6

or three weeks before it's in the shops, one of the very first in the whole country to have it. And what is Rex going to make us do? . . . Well, I think he's been fiddling with his tapes.

REX: I have indeed –

LEONARD: Very posh today aren't we, Rex?

REX: Are we, Leonard?

LEONARD: And what have you done with your tapes?

REX: I've slowed them down – rather a lot.

LEONARD: Slowed them down – we're getting even more posh.

REX: Yes.

LEONARD (*loud*): Tell me Rex, what effect does this have on the listener?

REX: What?

LEONARD (*very fast*): What effect does this have on the *listener*?

REX: What . . . well it . . . (REX *dries completely, stands helpless.*) I . . .

LEONARD *presses the button: a tape of the Leicester Sound jingle cuts off* REX's *floundering.*

LEONARD: Enough of this gibberish. (*Normal voice.*) OK, sweets – this is it. Rex is going to play one of the songs in the Top *Eleven*, and it has been slo-o-o-o-wed do-o-o-own, so it sounds a little different. And you're going to give us the singer and the song aren't you . . . Double five three zero four is the number to ring . . . that's right. (*Bogart voice.*) Play it again, Rex.

REX *back in his box, switches on a tape of 'The Proud One' by the Osmonds at 16 rpm.*

LEONARD (*after a few bars, reducing the volume on the*

monitor speakers, he talks into the intercom to REX; *off the air*.) Sounds a little more exciting like this doesn't it. I shall always play it like this in future. (*Suddenly loud*.) All records will be played at *eight* rpm, and we'll talk that slowly too.

REX *has come out of the box*.

REX: I'm . . . sorry about messing things up, I didn't mean to . . .

LEONARD: Of course you didn't –

REX: You took me by surprise, I didn't think . . . I'm sorry, I won't do it again.

LEONARD: No of course you won't. You won't get another chance to. Now get back into your box where you belong. (*He returns to the mike; switches it to go live again. Loud*.) Rex – what have you done to my favourite song? How's that for first-degree murder – a fine song slo-o-o-owly tortured to death. OK, sweets, who can be the first caller – race to your phones, dial furiously . . . I'm touching the first prize now – all fourteen tracks of it . . . we're handling the two of them with rubber gloves up here – and forceps, and we're keeping them in an incubator at night, in case we can hatch a third. Seriously now – (*He's put his headphones on*.) – we have a caller; and the first caller is . . .

A GIRL'S VOICE (*on the telephone, amplified through the monitors*): Hello? Hello . . .

LEONARD (*softly*): Hello there . . . what's your name, love?

GIRL: Angela . . .

LEONARD: Lovely. Have we ever talked before?

ANGELA: No, never –

LEONARD: Fine. You at home Angela?

ANGELA: Yeah – I'm at home.

LEONARD: Good – well, let's go straight into it Angela, into the unknown . . . (*Signalling to* REX, *who switches on the slowed-down tape again, in the background.*) Who do you think the noise is, this *slo-o-ow* noise?

ANGELA: Is it – 'The Proud One' by the Osmonds?

LEONARD: Did you say –

ANGELA (*about to correct herself*): I . . .

LEONARD: Angela, you're r-r-r-o-o-o-o-ight! Well done! (REX *speeds up the record to the right speed, it plays a few bars.* LEONARD *signals* REX *and the volume is reduced.*) There we go – clever girl. I'm dropping your prize into Rex's hand to be wiped spotless, and posted, jet-propelled towards you Angela. Bye, love. Let's have the next one Rex. (*A slowed-down version of 'I Can't Give You Anything* (*But My Love*)' *by the Stylistics.* LEONARD *gets up again.*) This is an easy kill for them – they use their record-players so much at home, they all run slowly anyway . . . those who *have* record-players.

REX (*staring at* LEONARD): I really like it, you know – (*Slight smile.*) – *if* I'm allowed to say so, how you always touch something when you're talking about it, even if it's the wrong record, like just now.

LEONARD: Yes. I like that too. It's the actor in me. It's what makes it reasonably good. (*Staring round the studio.*) Where is the nauseating object anyway? (*Sees the Yellow Jacks LP, picks it up.*) Have you read the back, with Ross – (*American voice.*) – the lead singer speaking *his mind.* (*Normal voice.*) Take an example at random – and this is a nice lad from Bolton speaking – 'Ross numbers among his favourite things: walnut ice-cream, honeysuckle, genuine people, starfish, and sunburnt bare feet.' (*Loud.*) You realise we're going to have to play the utterances of this jellied imbecile all this week – the

9

promoters have sent us a long tape, in a silk case, and the station's excited too, they want it to be a lively few days; I keep getting little illiterate messages from Johnson pushed under the door saying, 'Please remember, *maximum* required'. (*He switches on the mike suddenly.*) Hello – what's your name please?

GIRL'S VOICE: Rita.

LEONARD (slight smile): Lovely Rita, Meter Maid?

RITA: What?

LEONARD: A reference to years gone by, don't let it worry you, Rita. Have we talked before?

RITA: No.

LEONARD: You listen often –

RITA: Yes . . . yes I do.

LEONARD (*smiles softly*): Good, that's how it should be. Let's go straight into it then love, into the nitty gritty – who do you think it is?

RITA: I think it's – (*She gives the wrong title.*)

LEONARD: Well, Rita, you're wrong, I'm afraid.

RITA: No I'm not . . . am I?

LEONARD: I'm afraid so.

RITA: You sure? . . . (*Louder.*) I was certain. You –

LEONARD (*cutting her off*): I'm sorry love, you're wrong; keep listening though, for a very important reason . . . bye for now. (*Hughie Green voice.*) And let's go straight in to the next contestant! Coming up to Big John with the news at three o'clock. One down, one LP to go – round, crisp and shiny. What's your name please?

NICOLA'S VOICE (*extremely flat, unemotional*): Hello.

LEONARD: A little louder please – what's your name?

NICOLA (*very quiet*): Nicola Davies.

LEONARD: A little louder.

NICOLA (*loud*): Nicola Davies.

LEONARD: Nicola Davies. That's very formal. Are you at home, Nicola Davies?

NICOLA: Yes.

LEONARD (*suddenly interested*): And what are you wearing, Nicola?

NICOLA: Trousers . . .

LEONARD: A little louder – you've got a very nice voice, Nicola. You're wearing trousers, and anything else?

NICOLA: Yes . . . shoes.

LEONARD: Shoes, that's an interesting picture, she's wearing just trousers and shoes. Only wish we had television phones, sexy Nicola . . . so, to win this LP, that Rex is just slipping into its beautiful see-through tight-fitting sleeve – who is it, Nicola?

NICOLA: It's the Stylistics and – (*She gives the wrong title.*)

LEONARD: I'm afraid, Nicola . . .

NICOLA (*correcting herself*): No, it's 'I Can't Give You Anything (But My Love)'.

LEONARD: Well Nicola – I'm afraid your first answer is the only one I can accept . . .

NICOLA: Oh . . .

LEONARD: But you were very close – and so, as you've given us *all* your name, Nicola Davies – I'm going, actually, to give it to you.

NICOLA: Oh good – thank you.

LEONARD: Just for you, Nicola Davies, but on one condition – and that is –

NICOLA (*nervous*): What is that?

LEONARD: You listen for just one more moment, because I have something rather extraordinary to announce to everyone . . . I'm going to be running many competitions this week for all ages – but one of them is different – for, to tie in with the great Yellow Jacks' concert here

11

in this city on Saturday we're running THE COMPETI-
TION OF THE CENTURY . . . and the prize is actually
meeting one of the boys. How do you like that, Nicola
Davies?

NICOLA: Yes . . . what do you do?

LEONARD: And not only that – the winner will ride to
London, after the concert, in *their* car, sitting with *them*,
and what is more they will then spend four whole days in
London, the capital of this fine country, at the expense
of Leicester Sound. That's OK, isn't it? – Nicola?

NICOLA: Yes . . .what do –

LEONARD (*cutting it off*): So everybody tune in tomorrow,
for the first stage – you too Nicola – (*His voice quieter,
smiles.*) – you never know – what your luck might be –
we might even speak again. (*He puts down the phone.
Drops his biro onto the desk. Pause. Quiet.*)
    We're off.

Blackout.

Scene Two

In the blackout: a radio commercial.

SHARP TRANSATLANTIC VOICE: We are going DOWN!
DOWN! DOWN! Yes, everything's down at Liptons.
Shop at Liptons where eggs are down – (*Echo effect.*) –
DOWN! DOWN! Bacon is down and what's not down's
not up.

SONG: LIPTONS MAKES THE GOING EASY, LIP-
TONS MAKES THE GOING GREAT!

*As the song continues, there is a sudden explosion of
white light. Supermarket. The music of the commercial
breaks into pop music, playing in the background.*

NICOLA *standing by the fridge, staring ahead, pale face.*

SUSAN'S VOICE (*off-stage*): Nicola?

    NICOLA *doesn't react.* SUSAN *enters, stands at a distance from* NICOLA.

SUSAN: Nicola? Here . . .

    NICOLA *glances up. Suddenly* SUSAN *crosses over to the fridge, very sharply.*

NICOLA (*surprised, nervous*): What you doing over here?

SUSAN: What do you think?

NICOLA: You shouldn't have come over. You know you're meant to stick to your own counter.

SUSAN: Why should I? I hate standing over there, by myself all the time. I've got to talk to somebody, haven't I – even you! Anyway, I start thinking funny thoughts, after a bit. (*She glances up at the strip-lighting.*) If you stare at those lights long enough, it does that.

NICOLA (*sharp*): You'll be seen any moment, you know.

SUSAN: I won't. (*She feels her tunic.*) Christ, I'm tired after that rush, and it'll soon be starting again. (*Pulling at her tunic.*) I get so hot in this all over. What's that – let's see that . . .

NICOLA: Nothing.

SUSAN (*making a grab for it*): What you got a postcard for, with nothing on it.

NICOLA: Stop it! You'll get it wet. (*She puts the postcard back.*) Look, if I'm seen talking to you, by the camera – (*They both glance up.*) – we'll both get it, won't we? You just have to make a wrong move, and he'll see you, won't he?

SUSAN: Don't worry, I'm watching out. (*She smiles.*) It's coming now. (SUSAN *ducks.*) You know what happened yesterday? Something exciting. What do you think – a cat got in here, it did. Just after you'd gone. Came through the stacks of Ryvita up there, suddenly there it was. *In here!* You know, spitting and everything. I thought it was a Giant Rat, we all suddenly stopped what we were doing and rushed after it, shouting and screaming our heads off. It really got everybody going. You should have seen us. Made a change. Didn't last long – you missed it!

NICOLA: Yes.

SUSAN (*loud*): I wonder if anything else will get in here soon.

LEONARD BRAZIL'S VOICE (*suddenly piping up.*) That was – (*Title of record.*) Don't fear, Leonard Brazil is here. Hello there, wherever you are, whatever you're doing, and a special hello to you. (*As if to all the girls, but strangely personal.*) Yes, you down there, I'm saying hello to *you*.

NICOLA: He's quite loud today.

SUSAN: Yes, he is.

L.B.'s VOICE (*running on*): I've got a lot of goodies coming up, and no bad 'uns. Every sound is freshly picked up here, specially for you, that's why they're so ripe and full of flavour. Juicy! You don't believe me, well, it's true.

The music begins.

SUSAN: He's talking a lot today, isn't he?

L.B.'s VOICE: Very soon that special something I promised, Stage One . . .

NICOLA: Yes.

L.B.'s VOICE: Until then, let's move onto the year 2000 and maybe we'll be listening to this. (*He plays 'Long Haired Lover From Liverpool.'*)

SUSAN (*looking into the fridge*): I'm so hungry, aren't you,

14

can't stop feeling hungry.

NICOLA: Careful, what you doing. He'll kill us if he sees.

SUSAN (*her hand inside the fridge*): It's horrible inside here.
We could fuse this fridge, you know – just have to get the
right thing. (*She pulls at something inside the fridge.*)
Once saw it happen, all the food melts slowly, goes soggy
and bad, and it all floats in a big kind of mush, you can
pour the whole lot out like a lot of soup. (*She pushes the
fridge.*) It moves too, you see!

NICOLA: Don't, please . . . I don't want trouble today,
Susan . . .

SUSAN (*pushing the fridge*): It moves easily, we could push it
down there if we wanted.

NICOLA (*shouts*): Mind! (SUSAN *springs back as the camera
pauses. Nervous.*) He's seen us now. Think. You're
going to get us sacked at any moment now.

SUSAN: I wouldn't mind that – I wouldn't. Anyway, he's
asleep most of the time, the guy who watches it. Up in
the office.

NICOLA: No, he's not! When there aren't many customers,
like now, he's watching us all the time.

SUSAN: Yeah, he enjoys doing that. It's his sort of game.
Come on – (*She calls to the camera, then ducks.*)

NICOLA: Have you seen him yet. Do you know what he
looks like?

SUSAN: Yes, I saw him through the door once. He's very
fat. I've heard all about him, he sits there all day, with
one of his socks off, picking his toes, and eating the stuff,
while he watches.

NICOLA: He doesn't do that, does he?

SUSAN: Yes – he used to be a policeman, you know. And
when he sees a customer taking something, or one of us,
he has them up there, and he says 'He'll let them go'. If

he can do what he likes with them for half an hour, puts his hand down you know and that – (*She pushes her hand inside twice.*)

NICOLA: You're making all this up, like always.

SUSAN: I'm not. It's true! And that's why you stare so much at the camera, isn't it? Because you wanted to get noticed – be invited up there. You want that to happen, don't you?

NICOLA: I don't. Well, it might be interesting. But I don't just wonder about him!

SUSAN: Maybe he's staring at us, right at this moment, smacking his lips – about to jump. (*She looks into the fridge.*) Have you taken anything yet, then?

NICOLA: No.

SUSAN: Have you stopped taking things, then?

NICOLA: No, but they've started searching us, haven't they?

SUSAN: Yes. My mum doesn't believe they search us. She can't think why they should have to, except for bombs, in case we had bombs! (*She puts her hand into the fridge.*)

NICOLA: It's coming round again. Careful!

SUSAN: Nicola . . . let's take something now, right now.

NICOLA (*astonished*): What?

SUSAN: Come on – take that! (*She throws* NICOLA *some food.*) And that . . . and that . . . (*Throwing a huge bundle of food at* NICOLA.)

NICOLA: Look, stop it, Susan. Stop it, it's coming . . .

A large can drops out of her hands and rolls along the floor. At the same moment, the music cuts off. Silence. NICOLA *turns, frightened and bewildered, and rushes out in front of the fridge to pick up the can.*

ROSS'S VOICE: Don't move, folks, stay right where you are,

because yes, it's me. See you Saturday.

L.B.'s VOICE: Those few words were spoken by you know who, Ross. I'll be playing some more of his dulcet tones tomorrow.

NICOLA: Shhh! I want to really listen now.

L.B.'s VOICE (*strangely gentle, as if half-aimed at her*): So have you got a lead pencil ready – is it in your hand – are you gripping it – hold it – tight – won't you – because we've come to that moment you've been waiting for since yesterday . . .

SUSAN (*loud*): You're not going in for that competition, are you, you can't . . .

NICOLA: Sssh! Be quiet.

L.B.'s VOICE: Come on, now then, are you ready, because I'm only going to say it *once*, so pin back those ears of yours, and listen . . . ready . . .

Sudden silence.

NICOLA (*loud*): What's that . . .

Just silence.

NICOLA: They've switched it off.

SUSAN (*smiles, teasing*): Yes – they must have known what you were going to do.

NICOLA: They would switch it off then!

FAT MAN'S VOICE (*silky, nauseating, menacing*): Can Miss Lyle come into the office please . . . Could Miss Lyle come here immediately, please . . . immediately . . .

SUSAN (*loud, defiant*): It's not us . . . it's that old bag, seen her nicking . . .

NICOLA (*moving backwards and forwards*): They were only going to say it once, weren't they? How can I find it out?

SUSAN: You can't go in for *that* competition. You won the

17

record yesterday. They wouldn't even let you start.

NICOLA: I must find it out, probably won't be something like this for ages – where's the building that it comes from.

SUSAN: No idea. They'd never let you in, either.

NICOLA: No. (*She turns.*) I'll phone them up then. I know the number.

SUSAN (*smiling*): Can't use that phone. Only for supervisors.

NICOLA: I don't care. (*She moves.*)

SUSAN (*loud*): Mind! Nicola! (*The camera stops . . . the camera pauses . . .*) You'll never get over there without being seen. He's watching now. (NICOLA *stares across at the phone.*)

FAT MAN'S VOICE: Miss Lyle . . .

NICOLA: It's worth a try. I'm going to. (*She moves in front of the fridge, sideways, crouches, dashes furiously for the phone; one second pause, then she immediately starts dialling furiously, bending to keep her head down.*)

SUSAN (*calling across to her*): Keep down . . . down. You haven't got long now. Hurry!

We hear a very loud 'engaged' tone. NICOLA *slams the phone down and immediately starts dialling again.*

SUSAN: Probably hundreds of people trying – everybody. You won't get to speak to *him* again.

NICOLA: Sssh!

The very loud 'engaged' tone. NICOLA *slams down the receiver. Immediately she starts dialling again.*

SUSAN: It's coming round, Nicola. (NICOLA *is dialling furiously.*) You're going to get seen! (NICOLA *glances up, freezes as the camera passes.*) it's on you!

NICOLA (*staring up*): Go away . . . (*She finishes dialling:*

18

very very loud 'engaged' pips.) I hate that noise. (*She moves back to the fridge, not caring if she's seen or not.*)

SUSAN: There you are. I told you.

L.B.'s VOICE (*suddenly piping up*): What about that, then? What did you think of that. *Super, dooper* as they say in Russia. That was only the start, remember, wasn't it?

NICOLA: It would happen, wouldn't it?

L.B.'s VOICE: Of course I've been asked to repeat it, say it again for *you* that weren't listening, yes – I mean you. Which is against the rules, and I'll probably be fined an enormous sum of money and get banned for life, but I'm going to, just for you.

NICOLA: Hear that?

L.B: OK, sweet-s. Here's Stage One again. The First Great Stage, and it is: if you could go anywhere in the world you can think of, with one of the Yellow Jacks, which one would you choose, where would you go, and why. (*Jokey voice.*) You're not allowed to choose me, and the *thirty* best ones get through to Stage Two. That's not so difficult is it, in fact it's the easiest I could make it for you – isn't it? And now . . . (*Music starts. He cues the record.*)

SUSAN: Now you know, don't you?

NICOLA: Yes, leave me alone now.

SUSAN: Your postcard's filthy, you know.

NICOLA: Yes, but I can still write on it, can't I?

L.B.'s VOICE: Are you OK then? It' over to you. (*The music coming up loud.*) I'm waiting for you, aren't I? (*Music loud.*)

Blackout.

19

Scene Three

The studio. LEONARD BRAZIL *is standing by his desk. A record is playing silently. A spool of tape is going round – and we hear* LEONARD's *personal jingle over the speakers.*

JINGLE: LB . . . LB . . . LB . . . LB . . . LB . . . (*He turns the volume up.*) LB . . . LB . . .

    Behind him, MICK YOUNG, *17 years old, nervous manner, is dragging in four large sackfuls bulging with postcards.*

LEONARD (*flicks off the jingle, swings round*): What are you doing with those?

MICK (*very nervous*): I . . . I'm carrying them in here . . . Mr Brazil.

LEONARD: Nothing is allowed in here, you know that.

MICK: Yes . . . Mr Brazil.

LEONARD (*staring*): What are they?

MICK (*very nervous*): They're bags . . . I . . .

LEONARD: Yes?

MICK: Replies from the listeners. Rex is finishing sorting them . . . you see . . . and there're so many we thought you'd like to see them.

LEONARD (*casually*): Did you. (*He puts his hand into one of the bags, pulls out postcards.*) All these are replies, are they?

MICK: You really got them to write in all right, didn't you . . . Mr Brazil.

LEONARD (*slight smile*): I had a ridiculous dream about these girls last night, do you know that?

MICK (*nervously*): No . . . Mr Brazil.

LEONARD (*lightly*): I was in a small park. There was a whole line of them coming towards me – about twenty of them,

20

and they said they wanted to give me a present – a new pair of trousers, but could they first have my old ones to burn. They must have my old ones to burn immediately. (*He looks at* MICK.)

MICK (*bewildered*): Yes?

LEONARD (*turns, sharply, businesslike*): Come on, take these all out again – the whole lot at once.

MICK (*struggling to pick them up*): Yes, of course.

LEONARD: This place is meant to be the nerve centre of the city, isn't it. And you fill it with all this clobber. Go on, we have very little time.

He brings up the record volume and goes on the air. As he does so, REX *enters, stops* MICK *picking up the bags, and they both stand and watch* LEONARD *from the side. At the end of* LEONARD*'s piece over the air* MICK *leaves silently.*

LEONARD: That was Peters and Lee and 'Welcome Home'. And now I've got something to say, folks. (*Gentle tone.*) To all of you, I have a message from our little friends, the Po-Leese. They say a lot of people in this fine city of ours have been taking what doesn't belong to them. In plain full frontal language, *stealing* and our little friends in blue have had to go into schools and shops, and put down the deadly purple dye . . . so they can catch them purple-handed. So seriously now, I know times are hard, but keep out of trouble – you will, won't you? (*Tone changes.*) Very soon on this Wonderful Wednesday we have Big John with all the News In The World – till then, let's explode with a raving cataclysmic ditty from 1968, the Rolling Stones and 'Street Fighting Man'.

Explosion of sound. LEONARD *listens for a moment, sees* REX *and cuts it out suddenly.*

21

LEONARD: What you doing?

REX (*standing staring*): I was watching you.

LEONARD: That's not permitted, especially the amount you do. Your ogling is getting on my nerves. Why do you do it?

REX: Because it really interests me, doesn't it. (*Smiles.*) Have you heard anything from Capital? (*Fast.*) Do you think they're listening now and going to . . .

LEONARD (*sharp*): That, Rex, is a forbidden subject, and you know it is. Come on, we have three minutes to go.

REX (*still standing there*): Yes, Leonard . . . I wondered if . . . I just happen to have an item here I thought you might like or perhaps even . . .

LEONARD: You could have a quick spot and read it yourself? That's what you were going to say, wasn't it? You're pushing aren't you lad. I do believe you're beginning to *push*. I've never ever seen somebody begin so early.

REX: I'm not . . . I. (*Quick.*) I'll just read it, shall I? (*He takes out a black notebook.*)

LEONARD: That's the little notebook with all of Rex in it, that you keep hidden in your box.

REX: It's an absurd news item. (*He reads.*) 'And we've just heard that in a Walls factory in Luton, a severed leg was found in a vat of raspberry ripple ice cream. The authorities are checking to see if they've got a cone big enough for it.'

Silence.

LEONARD: Even from somebody like you, that is quite diabolically dreadful. You're a disgrace to this microphone. (*Suddenly looks him straight in the face.*) You are!

REX (*startled*): What do you mean? What's wrong with it? People like black jokes now – I've some *much* blacker ones, you know. They love them – can't have enough. It's what they really want.

LEONARD (*sudden*): You don't have to tell me what they want, Rex.

REX: No, of course not. (*Genuine admiration, quiet.*) I *know* you know.

LEONARD: That's better.

> BIG JOHN *enters; a shiny, red-faced man.*

JOHN: Hello there, everyone. (*Smiles.*) Two minutes to go.

LEONARD: The lad's being pushy.

JOHN: Is he? That's no surprise.

REX (*nervous suddenly*): I'm sorry, I didn't mean . . .

LEONARD: We've got to go on to Stage Two in two minutes, go on . . . get out! (*He switches onto the air without a break, fading down the record.*) Hello sweet-s – stand by. Very soon now you'll have you know what – till then, here's . . . (*He plays something very cheap and nasty. As soon as he's faded out, he swings round and cuts back like lightning into his talk with* REX, *who has left the studio.*)

LEONARD (*loud*): And you make one mistake, Rex, and you're fired – do you hear that? (*Quieter.*) That boy makes me nervous.

JOHN: I didn't know that was possible.

LEONARD (*flicks round, stares at* JOHN): You look particularly cheeful today, don't you, John?

JOHN: Thank you. I'm in very good form, yes.

LEONARD: As usual, you've probably got a train disaster and a couple of mass murders there – (*Tapping* JOHN'*s file.*) – and your cheeks are positively glistening – Bright and Rosy.

JOHN: Thank you. (*Smiles.*) But I haven't got anything really spectacular now – maybe by tea-time something will come in.

LEONARD (*slight teasing smile*): Good.

JOHN: What's this I've just heard about approaches from the Big Wide World, from the actual Capital Radio. Are they going to . . .

LEONARD: You didn't hear anything of the kind. (*Loud.*) *Nothing* of the kind.

JOHN (*startled*): I'm sorry, I didn't realize . . .

LEONARD: No, you don't, John. You see this. (*He picks up.*) This piece of paper – that is the *Competition of the Century*. (*He holds it up.*)

JOHN (*looking at it*): Yes, it's a real cash box week, this week, isn't it? One minute, fifteen seconds to go . . .

LEONARD: And you know what . . . (*He pauses.*) I've done something which I've never done before, John. I've picked out an average girl for this competition. Yes, I picked out her voice. I home in on her each time I go on the air, home in on that voice. And I imagine her face. It would be funny if she knew, wouldn't it?

JOHN (*hardly looking up*): Really?

LEONARD: In fact, each time I pass by the window, I half expect to see her – a small dot standing right down there, staring up towards here, her spectacles flashing – if she wears spectacles. (*He glances at* JOHN *who is not listening.*) You're the only one that knows that yet, John.

JOHN: Yes. I've got no tongue-twisters today, luckily. One minute to zero. Peppermint? (*He sucks one himself.*)

LEONARD: If there was an earthquake today, or a full-scale revolution, those girls wouldn't notice, not a chance. (*Abrasive.*) I taught kids that age once, years ago! But they weren't like this. (*He taps* JOHN's *file.*) Got any earthquakes locked in there?

JOHN: No thank goodness. Nothing like that.

LEONARD: Perhaps you should have.

JOHN (*suddenly looks up*): You must be enjoying all this anyway – it's your greatest week ever, isn't it?

LEONARD: Oh, I am. I am.

JOHN: After all, you've always been wonderful at whipping people up, getting them to TUNE IN. You only have to say the word . . .

LEONARD: Yes?

JOHN: Just have to breathe over the air. They're all waiting for you now.

LEONARD (*standing over controls*): That's right, John. Got your little furry mascot ready, have you? Go on, *hold it up!*

JOHN (*holds it so that* LEONARD *can see*): Yes, of course I have. Ten seconds to zero . . .

LEONARD: You dropped it yesterday in mid-sentence. Hold on to it very tightly, John. (*He flicks on the switch, fades out the music.*) That was the cuddly sound of – (*He gives the name of the record. His tone changes, becoming personal.*) We're coming to you very soon now, love, so don't fret, don't worry . . . It's three o'clock and here's Big John with all the News In The World.

> BIG JOHN *starts reading the News, world items of extreme unrest, mingled with local items. As he reads,* LEONARD *crosses to the far end of studio, out of microphone range, and calls out remarks to him, trying to put him off.*

LEONARD (*smiling*): You know, John, I don't seem to be able to believe anything you say today . . . I'm talking through the News, John . . . I think your mascot's going to fall . . . (*He begins to cross over towards him.*) Perhaps you need a tickle. (*He crosses to* BIG JOHN *who's reading the News unwaveringly and begins to tickle him under the chin, and then under the arms, in the ribs.* JOHN *shifts in his chair, but keeps reading.* LEONARD *crosses to his desk. Sharply.*) It's got no life in it.

JOHN (*on the air*): And now back to Leonard, and that Competition of the Century.

LEONARD: Our thanks to Big John for reading the News so nicely and so firmly. Stand by, love, any moment. (*Music plays. He fades it down.*)

JOHN: Somebody'll hear you one day, Leonard. Always jealous of people taking away your microphone, aren't you . . . even for a moment. Always trying to put them off . . .

LEONARD: Rubbish! Anyway, I never manage to . . . (*Suddenly really abrasive.*) *Competitions have an effect on me.*

REX (*entering loudly and suddenly with a trolley completely smothered in objects*): Here you are!

LEONARD (*facing him*): What are those?

REX: They're your bribes.

LEONARD (*sharp*): My what?

REX: Your bribes, Leonard – from the girls.

LEONARD (*completely surprised*): They sent all those? Why?

REX (*scrambling over the trolley*): They're hundreds of them. Watch – nicked from her dad, probably. A T-shirt with your initials on it, some cheese, some socks with toes, a whole cake with *you* on it, a walking stick, and lots of photos of themselves.

LEONARD (*staring at them, quiet*): All for me . . . ? (*He picks up the photos, stares at them.*)

JOHN (*moving over the the huge stack of bribes*): You're

doing very well out of this, aren't you? I don't know what you're worrying about. You're in the middle of a glorious week. (*Feeling objects, pouring over them.*) We've never had a response like this. Could live off this for a month. (*Casually.*) I wonder if there's anything there for me. (*He picks up the watch, or the cheese.*) I could do with this. (*He pockets it.*)

LEONARD: John! Go and find some more *News*. Something worth listening to, for once.

    BIG JOHN *goes.*

LEONARD (*urgent*): We're very late now. (*He glances down at the photos, then throws them on his desk.*)

REX (*looking at the photos*): What were you looking for?

LEONARD (*sharp*): Nothing. I wasn't looking for anything. (*Slight smile.*) What am I going to make them do next, then?

REX (*astonished*): *I* don't know. (*Excited, smiling.*) It could be so many things . . . It's got to be something they can photograph for Saturday's front page.

LEONARD: Christ! Look at you, grinning all over your face. You're as bad as Johnson and all the rest upstairs – not that they ever are upstairs, given half the chance. They'd have the kids tunnelling under the motorway, or buying eighty 'Leicester Sound' T-shirts each before being allowed to win.

REX: Yes – they will do absolutely anything, those kids. They're desperate just to get into the studio and meet you, and then the Yellow Jacks and everything as well!! The last concert the Yellow Jacks did here, a girl asked Ross, begged him to sign her lip. I saw it, and he did and I wondered if she was going to cut that bit off and keep it in a jam jar, so the signature wouldn't come off.

LEONARD: Stop that – you're not going to talk like that in here – understand! *I don't like it. (He switches on music, goes onto the air.)*

REX (*as* LEONARD *does so*): I'm sorry, Leonard.

LEONARD: Hello, sweet. How are you then? Good. I wish you could see the sight up here. The studio is brimming with your answers, they're hanging everywhere. Rex is just handing me the postcards – perhaps *your* postcard, enabling you to get through to Stage Two. Hurry, Rex! Had a hard job sorting them, have you, Rex?

REX (*entering into the double act*): Yes, Leonard. We've been simply wading through entries.

LEONARD: Up to your knees, were you?

REX: Up to our stomachs in some places, up to our mouths, Leonard . . .

LEONARD: You nearly drowned our Rex, love. Pity you didn't send a few more. (*He begins to read the cards briskly.*) Diane Williams of 30 Sutton Road says she'd like to go to Scotland with Peter and climb mountains with him because he's afraid of heights. Quite a sadist, aren't you, Diane. Thank you for that. Pam Lawrence of 10 Rosendale Avenue says she'd like to go to London with Ross, because that's what the real prize is. I like that, a real realist, there. Pam will go far, won't she. Linda Perry of 18 Horseley Road says she'd like to go to the moon with Ross, that's a long way to go, Linda. Because he looks so like an astronaut, and Nicola Davies of 35 Poole's Road – rather a grubby postcard isn't it, Nicola – says she'd like to go to Kenya with Ken, that's a Nicola-type joke, and go on safari because Ken looks so good in a suntan and so I'm sure, would you, Nicola. You're through *all the way* to Stage Two now, love, and a list of all those that have qualified. Get your lead pencil ready . . . (*Music is playing.*)

REX (*nervously*): What happens if we don't think of something, Leonard?

LEONARD: What indeed, Rex. (*Slight smile.*) Disaster.

REX: Perhaps some sort of race . . .

LEONARD: There is of course something staring us in the eyeballs *right at this moment*! Isn't there?

REX (*staring at the desk*): What?

LEONARD: It isn't original. It's been used in America several times. (*He picks up the T-shirt.*)

REX (*excited*): What is it?

LEONARD: And it's rather cheap, not what they're used to.

REX (*louder*): What is it?

LEONARD: They might just enjoy it. *Just.*

REX: What is it, Leonard?

LEONARD (*swings round*): And it is: they have to make a portrait dummy of Ross, or any of the others, *life size*.

REX: What?

LEONARD: A model, effigy. A dummy of one of the Jacks, out of old clothes, like a guy, stuffed full and life size. That's the idea, Rex.

REX: That's . . . that's pretty good, in fact, it's brilliant. (*Loud.*) It is.

LEONARD: It's not at all. It's not even good, but it'll *just* do.

REX (*quiet*): It's great.

LEONARD (*by the controls*): Christ – listen to that.

REX: What?

LEONARD: You can almost hear all their small ears pressed against the radio waiting for it. The Competition of the Century. (*He brings up the theme music really loud.*)

REX: You knew the answer all the time, Leonard, didn't you?

LEONARD: Rex is coming over with all of Stage Two in his

hands.

REX: Here it is, Leonard – all of it. (*He hands him nothing.*)

LEONARD: Thank you, Rex. (*His tone suddenly personal, almost gentle.*) OK, *love*, what we want – what I want you to do *love*, is very simple and a little special, for the next stage of our remarkable obstacle race to get to the Yellow Jacks and London Town, where everything is still possible. I want you *love*, to make in the next two days, a model of one of the boys – (*Laughs.*) – one of the great Yellow Jacks, a model of Ross, or Dave, or Ken, or Pete. 'What do you mean, Leonard, make a model, a dummy, how on earth do I do that, Leonard – that's impossible!' Well, *love*, what you do is you get some old clothes, and paper and stuff it up him, right up and copy his face from a picture, and use some wool for his hair, or go to a gentleman's hairdresser, or even a ladies'. (*Gentle voice.*) 'Please could I borrow your shavings?' No, seriously, *love*, don't spend any money on it, and get it to me at Leicester Sound by five o'clock Friday. Do you understand now, love? And the two who make the most wondrous accurate models will become the finalists, and come up here. That can't be bad. It's not. So do your best, *love*, and hurry, won't you. Good hunting.

A blast of music, as he brings in a record.

LEONARD (*Very abrasive*): *I don't like competitions!*

Music up again.

Blackout.

Scene Four

NICOLA*'s room. Radio playing in the background.* NICOLA *pulling out a pile of magazines methodically from under* *the bed and from the side of the room, and a pile of cans, packets, etc. that she's taken from the supermarket.* SUSAN *watching.*

SUSAN: I don't want to stick around. Don't know why I should.

NICOLA: You said you would. (*She continues to pull stuff out into the room.*)

SUSAN: What you doing with all of this?

NICOLA: There's not much time.

SUSAN (*suddenly grabbing a poster from the pile*): Hey! you've got one of these. Who's it of? (*She unfolds an enormous pin-up poster of a star, holds it up and looks at it.*) Oh, him! You haven't done it, have you? Don't you know the point? (*She lays it out on the floor.*) Got it at shop, did you, off the market . . . They're from America . . . Don't you know what to do? You have to wet it. (*She lies down on top of it.*) Wet it with anything you've got and rub it all over. Rub.

NICOLA (moving over to her): Yes. (*She rubs hastily too.*) We haven't got time, really.

SUSAN: And the top should sort of peel away. (*She is lying on top of the poster.*) And you see all the hair underneath, and you see *everything.* (*She rubs, still lying on the poster.*) It's not really his body, it's somebody else's and they cut his head off. (*Loud.*) Come on! (*She rubs frantically.*) It's too old! (*Loud.*) It doesn't work! (*She rubs again. Loud.*) Why not. I *wanted* it to.

NICOLA: Probably never did work. Come on – I've lost time now. Hurry!

SUSAN (*lying on the poster*): I took one of these to sex education class, she was new then, Miss Booth, thought she'd be interested. She hit me across the face! Right there! Girls shouldn't have such things and all that. Why not? I saw her flushing it down the toilet, she talked like a dalek, anyway. I couldn't hear any of her sex education lessons, the traffic noise right by me. (*Loud.*) I never heard *anything* at school.

LEONARD BRAZIL'S VOICE (*on the radio*): That was – (*Name of record.*) How are you doing then? Yes, I mean *you*, whoever you are, wherever you are, you with the sticking out ears. That's right, keep it up, you haven't got long.

NICOLA: Yes. (*She works even faster collecting all the objects together ready for the stuffing.*)

SUSAN: He's hurrying you now.

L.B'S VOICE (*continuing straight on*): Rex's bulky shape is beside me here in the studio as always (*Sudden mock surprise.*) Hey, he's moving away now, don't leave me, Rex, don't leave me. He's going. How can you do this to me, he's left me. I'm alone and afraid Raindrops might start falling on my head – (*Tone changes.*) – and yours too.

    Music begins. 'Raindrops Keep Falling On My Head.'

NICOLA: You know, I think he liked me a bit or something when I rang in . . . He spoke to me longer than the others, different.

SUSAN: He only spoke to you different from the others because he was waiting for the News to come up.

NICOLA (*to herself*): Ready now! (*Worried.*) I'm running out of time, come on! (*She suddenly pulls the dummy out from under the bed, all in pieces, the huge torso, the decapitated head, the hands, the feet, the arms, etc.*)

SUSAN: Look at it! You'll never finish that in time.

NICOLA: Got to. Got to fill it up, make it stiff.

SUSAN (*picking up some of the supermarket objects*): What are these?

NICOLA: Things I've taken from the shop, things I've nicked. They're all going inside. No use to me. I'm sending them all in this.

SUSAN (*picking up a pot of paint*): How did you get all this paint?

NICOLA: Saved lunch money.

SUSAN (*startled*): What have you been eating?

NICOLA: Haven't. Don't need to. So I go for days without eating if I have to. And can.

SUSAN: You'll starve to death, you will. (*Suddenly she picks up the head and a foot.*) Is this Ross?

NICOLA: Yes. He's the easiest to do, his face is very simple.

SUSAN (*suddenly loud*): He's very big.

NICOLA: Yes, I made him big. So he'd notice it.

SUSAN: We can do anything we want with him, now all his bits are here. We can stand on his face. (*She stands on it.*) Can't we? Pull his tongue out. (*She picks up the torso.*) Pull his knickers off . . .

NICOLA (*loud*): Don't do that, Susan. You'll tear him – it'll tear.

SUSAN: Yes! (*Firm.*) You're really stupid, do you know that? Even if you get this ready and Leonard just happens to pick it out, which he won't, even then you haven't really started. He can go on forever with you if he likes, *on* and *on* and *on*.

NICOLA (*determined*): I know that . . .

L.B.'S VOICE (*suddenly piping up*): Hello, how are you doing. Yes, I mean *you*, yes you, with the popping eyes and sticking out ears.

They both suddenly stop and stare at the radio.

L.B.'s VOICE: I hope I'm not interrupting *you*, am I, because a lady wrote to me to say she had the radio on when, lucky lad, she was giving birth to a baby son, Dominic, and the first sound Baby Dominic heard on this earth was yours truly's ugly grating tones pouring out. I'm getting worse and worse, aren't I? Stop polluting British steam radio – Great belches of grey filth pouring out of my mouth, straight at you down there. In a moment I'll be talking to John Robinson, who's just come out of the army and Northern Ireland and all the old troubles, and he's come home to talk to me.

During this speech, SUSAN *has crossed to the wireless and picked it up right at the beginning of* LEONARD'*s speech and turned the volume down. Then she sings loudly above it.*

SUSAN: Hear him. (*She holds the radio up with* LEONARD'*s voice pouring out of it.*) That's the nearest you'll get to him . . . this! It is not any nearer than that! (*She puts the radio down next to* NICOLA, *having turned the volume up.*)

L.B.'s VOICE: And now *you, you* down there who have entered the Competition of the Century, time is running out. Here's some music for you. (*Music begins.*)

NICOLA: Yes! Quick. (*She speeds up the stuffing of the dummy with the supermarket objects.*) You're going to help now.

SUSAN: No, I don't think I want to, now.

NICOLA (*swings round*): *You've got to!*

Pause.

SUSAN (loud): Why?

NICOLA: Because I'm going to get there. Into the building

34

and see him.

SUSAN (*quiet*): You won't . . .

NICOLA: Come on, there's no time at all now. Paint that yellow, quick!

SUSAN: If I have to . . . (*She takes a big brush and splashes huge dollops of yellow paint on the dummy's body. NICOLA stuffs the legs.*) Your room's too small, it'll stink of paint for evermore. You won't be able to live in here anymore.

NICOLA: Good. I want that. Hurry . . . paint.

SUSAN (*sploshing bright yellow paint on the torso. Gradually her paint strokes get faster and faster*): When they played at Coventry, Ken had a blue belt, the others had yellow as usual. I don't like this colour, sort of sick-looking. They ought to change it. You know I had to get back after the concert – it was twelve or after in the night.

NICOLA (*to herself*): Come on . . . (*She stuffs the legs and the head.*)

SUSAN: I didn't think I could get back. It was raining really hard, straight in your eyes. I got onto the road, started hitching – all these huge lorries went past, enormous. Looked much bigger in the dark. And you know, they all had their radios on. Yes! I could hear. It was Leonard Brazil. It was. He was coming from every single lorry. But none of them stopped.

NICOLA (*quiet, determined*): Come on, quick.

SUSAN (*painting fast*): So I *stood straight* in front of one of them and waved, and he *had* to stop, or flatten me, and he stopped all right, and he opened his door, all smiling and everything, and I got in, and you know what, the seat next to him was still warm, it was all covered with chocolate. Somebody had been sitting there just a moment before – *a girl.*

NICOLA (*to herself*): Faster.

SUSAN: I knew he was going to kill me then, yes, on the motorway, in the dark, on the side, where nobody could see, you know, get me on my back and jam a stick of lipstick down my throat, and I'd hear Leonard Brazil on the radio, and suddenly it'd stop, and I'd be dead, and they'd find me in pieces like this – (*Indicating the dummy as she paints.*) – in a bundle, in the mud, been assaulted, flies in my eyes, and all that. And pictures of me on the telly, me being lifted up and wrapped in a sheet, you know. (*Lightly.*) But nothing did happen. Nothing at all. (*Pause. She stops painting. Lightly.*) *I wanted it to.*

NICOLA (*suddenly very loud*): Oh! Look Susan, it's still not nearly full. (*She stares at the legs and then into the torso.*) We've got to fill it up now . . . (*Moving about, agitated.*) Now!

SUSAN: Put this in anyway. (*She crumbles the huge centrefold picture of the pop star. As she does so, they both suddenly look up with a jolt and stare at all the posters and ornaments in the room. The same idea hits them both.*)

NICOLA (*loud*): Yes! Come on. Everything . . .

They suddenly tear down all the posters and ornaments – everything in the room – and throw it into the stomach of Ross. The action begins swiftly and ends furiously. It lasts under a minute.

NICOLA (*as they do it*): Come on down.

SUSAN (*joyful*): Yes. It's coming down. What's that poster? Come on. (*And* SUSAN *rips it down.*)

NICOLA *takes everything off the chest of drawers, all her furry ornaments . . . everything.*

NICOLA: He's got to *be* full.

SUSAN (*loud*): Yes.

SUSAN's pent-up violence comes out in her attack on the posters, whereas NICOLA is more methodical, but also very fast. The music on the radio ends. They strip the room.

L.B.'s VOICE (*his tone very personal*): Hello there how's it going, then . . . Yes, *you?* You down there . Keeping at it, are you, *love*, that's good. (*He brings up more music or a commercial.*)

NICOLA (*throwing in objects*): Go on . . . in . . . in . . . in . . .

SUSAN: Come on down. (*She pulls the lightshade off and throws it in.*)

They are both exhausted. The outburst ends, the torso is full. NICOLA lifts it up. They both stare at it.

NICOLA: It's finished.

Blackout.

Scene Five

The studio. Night. A phone-in programme. The voice of a caller, JIM, about forty, on the telephone, coming out of the monitor speakers. The receiver of the telephone is off, lying on the desk. LEONARD BRAZIL is standing some distance away, at the back of the studio, smiling and listening.

JIM's VOICE (*heard first in the blackout*) . . . I mean, don't you agree with me Leonard, about these vandals, hooligans, whatever you like to call them, I mean, everywhere I go I actually *see* things being smashed up, I see them doing it, and writings things up. I mean, I saw some young thugs – I don't want to use abusive terms, especially on your programme, Leonard, and I certainly won't do so, but these men – they weren't just boys, they were grown men, and they were standing round this flower bed of red tulips, and they pulled up every single one, they were pulling them out, by the roots, and treading them into the ground . . . the whole lot . . .

LEONARD (*flicks off the switch to cut off the caller in mid-sentence. Silence. He smiles*): Why do they ring me, explain me that, why don't they phone each other . . .? (*He flicks the switch on again.*)

JIM'S VOICE: . . . and even more. And apart from that, I don't know if you find this, I mean as an important person, and obviously on the air – but I mean – these filthy phone calls – people ringing me up.

LEONARD (*turns the volume down, speaks to* REX *again through the intercom*): Is he going to start being rude – I think he is. Thank God I only have to do this twice a week – (*He turns the volume up again.*)

JIM'S VOICE: . . . you see what I mean, I don't want to mention anything filthy over the air of course – (LEONARD *holds his finger ready to press the cut-off button.*) – and I'm not going to, but I'm always getting wrong phone calls, people talking to me about things I don't know *anything about*! You know the feeling of course, being a famous person Leonard – somebody rang me the other day, started talking about my horse, how he wanted to buy it, get hold of it, I mean I don't have a horse. (*Loud.*) What would I do with a bleeding horse? (*Suddenly very loud.*) What would I do with a fucking horse in this fuck- (LEONARD *cuts him off.*)

LEONARD (*smiling, very calm*): I'd like to say goodnight now, Jim, thanks for that call, it was a Jim-type call. The time is 9.23 on the LB night show on this Competition Friday in Competition Week, so *hold on tight, love.* It's raining up here, raining black buckets just outside, so let's take a dip into the soft inside of Nostalgia Corner, go back to the golden days of 1967 when London was alive and wriggling and bursting at the seams, remember? Or perhaps you don't. And we were listening to this – some of us were –

    Music. 'See Emily Play' by the Pink Floyd. The volume is turned down after a few bars. LEONARD *takes off his headphones.*

LEONARD: That's enough. I don't want any more calls – you've already put through too many. (*He gets up.*) I hate that smell of new paint from the corridors.

    REX *enters from the box.*

LEONARD (*loud*): And *also* I've decided I'm not going to do my spot tonight.

REX: What do you mean? Why not?

LEONARD: I have reasons. Got to cope with Stage Three. (*Loud.*) I'm not doing it. That's final!

REX: Some people tune in specially for it. I mean you must do it this week of all weeks . . . we've never had so many calls, so many entries . . . if you would . . . it would . . .

LEONARD: I should, should I? No. (*He gets up, starts searching for something.*) I've never liked them . . . has anyone ever shown you this? The secret of phone-in's! Where is it . . . this . . . (*He starts pulling something out of a drawer.*) When we started, a colleague made these . . . (*Loud.*) Come on out! (*He pulls really hard. A huge*

39

mass of tapes, tangled, without their spools, in an enormous ball, comes out of the drawer.) Tapes. (*He pulls more out.*) Of the phone-ins, hundreds of them – see? (*He holds them up – a vast amount.*) There are a lot more around us, cupboards full, we should tie ourselves up in it, miles and miles of complaints and shouts and whimpers. (*He holds a piece of tape tight.*) And *frustration*! (*He runs his finger down the tape.*) You half expect to get scalded by them. He edited them, of course, to make them even more comical, more juicy – this disc jockey did.

REX (*smiling*): Great . . . I must listen to them sometime.

LEONARD: The usual Rex response. Take the whole lot – (*He tosses the mass of tapes at him.*) – they can become your bedtime listening, can't they.

REX (taking armful of tapes): There –

LEONARD (*pauses. He suddenly stares at* REX): You realise we're almost alone in this building, we're surrounded by empty corridors. You and me. That's a terrifying thought. I usually have my rest from you at this time.

REX: I know. I asked to do extra time specially.

LEONARD: Did you. (*Staring at him.*) You know, you're the most ambitious thing on three legs I've ever seen.

REX: That's not true. I only want to hang on to my job, don't I? I only want to become good at it.

LEONARD: Only that? I don't believe it?

REX: And I enjoy working on your show, of course.

LEONARD: Don't try to tell me that's the only reason for this fantastic obsessional attempt at efficiency.

REX: Yes, of course.

LEONARD (*smiles*): No it's not.

REX (*quiet*): Of course, eventually I want to get on . . . that's natural, isn't it? (*Smiles.*) I want my voice up in lights, eventually.

LEONARD (*quiet*): That's very good, Rex . . . for you.

REX (*unblinking*): It's your expression.

LEONARD (*surprised*): Is it?

REX: I heard it over the air, before I was working here. I *still* listen to you all the time. I even sit and listen to you at home, on my days off, when you're on.

LEONARD (*astonished*): You don't really do that, do you?

REX: Yes. (*Smiles lightly.*) There's nothing you've said that I don't remmeber, nothing! I've noticed everything that you've used up here. (*Smiles.*) I'm sort of photostating you really – all the time.

LEONARD (*slight smile*): So that's what you're doing. I wish you'd stop it. (*Moving away from him.*) You know what you are, Rex, you're reptilian.

REX: Yes.

LEONARD: Don't you ever let yourself go – go for a night on the town?

REX: No, neither do you. Do you?

LEONARD: You ought to get yourself another job – I mean that – and quick.

REX: Why should I? This is better than anything else I could be doing. I'd be out of work if I was down there. I want to be different, not a crime is it? And after all you're good aren't you? You are. In fact, Leonard, you could actually be the greatest, the best DJ there's ever been. Couldn't you? Yes, I mean singers become famous one day and are gone the next, but DJs go on and on. You will Leonard – I wonder what the people from Capital are thinking. You must have got it.

LEONARD (*loud*): I told you not to. (*He flicks a switch.*) 9.26 on the LB night show in Competition Week. We all had a great time at the open air concert last week, didn't we –

it was a true festival, a celebration if ever there was one – the greatest. But I've been asked to point out by the little man in blue – we did leave rather a mess, didn't we. It was six feet high in some places; the farmer couldn't find his sheep, or his bullocks – they were totally smothered, and he had a job locating his lady wife, found her under a pile of toilet paper and cigarette ends. Seriously, friends, let's try to be cleaner next time it'll save a lot of hassle. It's black and soaking wet out now, pelting towards us. Next, the results of Stage Three – stand by, *love*, this is it, now, after something from the summer of '67 when those topless young things with shining kneecaps bounced down the hot streets of our glorious London.

Music: 'A Whiter Shade of Pale' by Procol Harum. It continues to play under dialogue, quietly.

LEONARD: Come on. Bring them in. We'd better get this over.

REX: Yes. (*He doesn't move.*) You're playing a lot of oldies tonight.

LEONARD: Yes. (*Abrasive.*) I'm in a sentimental mood, aren't I? You're much too young to remember, of course.

REX (*smiles, looks innocent*): Too young to remember what, Leonard?

LEONARD: What do you think? (*Abrasive.*) Remember before the rot set in. I'm not in any way nostalgic about that time.

REX (*smiling, watching him*): Oh no?

LEONARD: No I'm not. I'm certainly not one of those mooning leftovers wallowing backwards all the time.

REX: No. Of course not.

42

LEONARD: I know exactly what it was like. (*Loud.*) Exactly.

REX: Yes.

LEONARD (*staring straight at him*): But it's undeniable, Rex,
that the music we were producing on that label, seven or
eight years ago, was *alive*. That is incontestable. It had
gut, it was felt, and it kicked, sometimes savagely. (*He
smiles, more flip.*) Because, of course, everything
seemed possible. (*Pause. He smiles.*) I was even quite
militant in a quiet way. (*Smiles.*) We thought things were
changing and all that romantic crap.

REX (*smiles*): Of course you did.

LEONARD: Don't stand there with that idiotic grin on your
face!

REX (*doesn't move*): No.

LEONARD (*smiles*): You'd better get on with it, hadn't you,
before I decide to take revenge.

   REX *goes.* LEONARD *talks to him as* REX *prepares
offstage.*

LEONARD: You should have been at the open air concert at
the weekend. *It was vile.* It was a perfect example.
(*Smiles, slightly mocking.*) A grey shabby echo of the
time when festivals really were celebrations. Everybody
was lying about in lifeless heaps, mumbling apologet-
ically, and getting bitten by horseflies. A few of them
were even fighting with each other in the mud. You felt
you could have turned them over with your foot, and
they wouldn't have been able to get up. I saw one girl, a
large girl, with a very big face, she wasn't very young,
wandering through a patch of long grass. Her face and
also her lips were sort of swollen, and completely ashen,
almost blue, in fact, as if was actually physically dead. I
almost wanted to go up and touch her; I felt that if you

touched that face it would probably flake into nothing. (*Smiles.*) In fact I haven't got that picture out of my mind yet.

    LEONARD *puts on another record in the current top ten. The sound of the record explodes through the speakers as the dummies are brought in.*

REX (*enters smiling with twenty-five dummies on a trolley, piled high*): You've got to make the final choice.

LEONARD: I don't believe it. (*Pause.*) I just don't believe it!

REX (*smiling unconcerned*): What's the matter?

LEONARD: You mean they did it – they actually made them?

REX: Yes, of course.

LEONARD: Dressed and everything?

REX: You didn't expect them to give us nude models, did you? Though they would have if you'd told them to.

LEONARD (*picks one up*): We could be in Los Angeles, couldn't we – except it's even worse. Christ, look, they've even painted fingernails on them, bound to be toenails under that. (*He pulls at their shoes, pulls at their hair.*) Probably their own new clothes too – or their little brother's. They must have worked all through the night on these obscenities. They're burrowing like moles to get up here! Why do they do it – tell me, why?

REX: Because you told them to do it.

LEONARD: You could drop anything over the air into that pool and they'd gobble it up. (*He feels one.*) What have they got inside them – feel this – feels as if it's stuffed with cans, and packets of frozen food! And all their magazines – clogged with them! How many of these ghastly objects are there?

REX: Twenty-eight. Two of them by people we'd eliminated at Stage One, but they still went and made them.

44

LEONARD (*has picked up another*): This is rapidly becoming a madhouse. We're being invaded by all these. Are they all there?

REX: All the best ones. I put some in the canteen – they're propped up in chairs – as a joke when people come in tomorrow.

LEONARD: AS *a joke*? (LEONARD *looks at the labels on the dummies, looking for* NICOLA'S.)

REX (*innocent smile*): Nothing wrong with that is there? I've put two in the ladies' toilet as well, sitting on the pan. So which two are you going to have – these are the best. Don't mind the paint on some of them, it got into their hair as I was pulling them along the corridor.

LEONARD: What?

REX: Which two are you going to choose . . . ?

LEONARD: These two'll have to do.

REX (*looks at the cards*): Louise Prentiss and Jane Harris. A good choice.

LEONARD: All right, get hold of them quickly, get this dealt with and . . . (*He suddenly looks up.*) Whose is that one?

REX (*looks at the card*): Nicola Davies.

LEONARD: Really – Nicola Davies. I thought so. Well let's have her instead shall we. Scrub that one?

REX: Why – you chose the other one.

LEONARD: Do as you're told.

> *Pause.*

REX: Have you got a thing about her or something?

LEONARD (*looks up*): No! Of course not. (*Pause.*) I picked her voice out, that's all. I've been using it. (*He looks at the dummy.*) They look more and more like home made corpses – take them away.

REX: They'll make pretty good photos in the paper

45

tomorrow, anyway.

LEONARD (*looks up*): I don't like that.

REX (*looks up*): What?

LEONARD: I don't like it do you hear? You ought to have stopped me thinking of it.

REX: *I* should have . . .

LEONARD (*really working himself up*): What do you think you're paid for? I mean this idea was trash. It was unpleasant!, incompetent, lazy – (*He throws the dummy down.*) – it's trash.

REX: Why?

LEONARD: If you can't see that there's no hope for you!

REX (*smiles*): No hope for me is there?

LEONARD: I need somebody that's going to think, *think*, don't I –

REX: Yes, Leonard, I –

LEONARD: Not just a callous, unquestioning, secret police vegetable . . .

REX: It isn't my fault . . .

LEONARD (*carrying on – a real outburst*): You'd be one of the first to come and take us away, wouldn't you. *Wouldn't you.* Come here.

REX: It was your idea Leonard.

LEONARD: You're an abortion really, aren't you – with absolutely no imagination. Nothing! A complete abortion.

REX (*loud*): I didn't think of it, Leonard, did I – it wasn't me –

LEONARD (*cutting him off*): You're a bloody idiot aren't you.

REX: It wasn't me, Leonard – was it.

LEONARD: Get out of here, go on.

REX *doesn't move.*

LEONARD: Go on, get out.

REX *moves out quickly*.

LEONARD (*shouting*): You're fired. Fired! You really are this time. I don't want to see you in this room again. You leave tomorrow. (*Complete silence for a moment. He faces the record desk and fades out the record*.) That was the Loving Spoonful and 'Summer in the City', and *this is* the Competition of the Century. And now we have come to that solemn moment – the finalists – the two people who are going to come all the way up here. Gauleiter Rex has written the two names out in red ink – you all did so well – showed enormous determination – the greatest in England. But the two who got through – the two names on the card are – Jane Harris and Nicola Davies. Jane and Nicola have won through to the Final. (*Fanfare. It fades down*.)

REX (*quiet, matter of fact, over the intercom*): I can only get one of them, Mr Brazil, the other one has gone to bed, she must have been very confident . . . I've got Nicola Davies for you.

LEONARD: Put her through then, Rex. (*He fades out the fanfare*.) Hello there Nicola Davies.

NICOLA'S VOICE (*over the monitor, quiet*): Yes, hello.

LEONARD: Hello there Nicola – I don't know if you've been listening to your radio – but I've rung to tell you, in front of the listening thousands, that you have reached the Final, the final round, of Competition of the Century –

Pause.

NICOLA (*flat, unsurprised*): Have I . . . Oh good.

LEONARD (*louder*): Did you ever think you could make it,

47

Nicola?

NICOLA (*matter-of-fact*): No.

LEONARD: Are you tall or short, Nicola?

NICOLA: Not tall, quite short.

LEONARD: That's funny. Rex said you were tall, I said you were short – you've got a short voice. What are you wearing now, love – what is Nicola wearing?

NICOLA: I'm wearing . . . I'm wearing a belt and top and trousers . . . and no shoes.

LEONARD: No shoes. (*Pause.*) I see. Ross'll like that. I'm looking forward to meeting you, Nicola Davies, tremend-ously. Aren't you?

NICOLA: Yes, I am. I am, Leonard . . . (*Flat.*) . . . very much.

LEONARD: Good . . . that's good. Nicola's going to be coming up here – I'm sure we'll get on. Tomorrow's going to be an extraordinarily good day, isn't it? There'll be some big surprises, I'm sure, and there's a big surprise now – do you usually stay to listen to the LB spot?

NICOLA: Oh, yes.

LEONARD: Well, Nicola, I have news for you. You are in it, you are in the LB spot. For each week, for those of you who have never listened before, and if there are any they'll be hung, drawn, and fined – LB has his spot, when he unleashes a few things. Are you still there, Nicola?

NICOLA: Yes. I'm here.

LEONARD: Well, you're high up, high up in the LB spot – high in the clouds. And the first – the first LB moment is, it's my birthday today, so I'm told, which is a lie because it's at least two years until my next birthday, and our friend Rex – who is definitely getting ideas – has made a cake. A cake out of melted down records. I have in front of me – (*He puts a book in front of him.*) – a pile of records squashed together with a cherry on top, thank you Rex, that's just the type of cake I deserve. (*Loud, runny voice.*) I deserve it – what am I saying? (*American.*) What's gone wrong with him? Seriously, folks I've been thinking about London, for a number of enormous reasons – London, capital of this fine country of ours. And of course it's the prize in the Competition of the Century. (*Fast.*) I was walking along Carnaby Street the other day, Nicola, it shows how old I am, I can pronounce that name correctly, yes I was there – I was Lord Kitchener's Grand-daughter – the street that made the world swing – you should see what it looks like now – it looks like a museum street, it needs its glass case – especially as half of it has been knocked down. The Americans, I hear, are going to ship it off soon across the seas – it'll be our last export, our swinging relics. They're shipping it off to Texas to stand in the desert somewhere, where it'll ooze away under the midday sun. (*Smiles.*) We mustn't get bitter! (*Funny voice.*) Your mouth tastes bitter, Brazil, it's going black round the edges. Remember where you are. You can't let the side down like this, Brazil. It's an important moment. Brazil, what are you doing? (*Quieter.*) What does he think he's doing? No . . . seriously everybody, London's still an exciting place – the most exciting place. The only place to be. It's still brown and beautiful. Why brown – why not? Mustn't get obsessed by all our yesterdays, they're gone thank goodness, must get obsessed by all our tomorrows. (*Like a machine.*) Hear hear. Hear hear. Hear hear. Don't spit on the animals. I said, don't spit on the animals – where's Nicola Davies – where is she? Still there, Nicola?

NICOLA: Yes, Leonard, I'm still here.

49

LEONARD (*smiles*): The rain is slashing at the window. I'm afraid, Nicola, if it gets to me I may melt . . . I'm afraid. Hear that, Nicola?

NICOLA: Yes. I heard.

LEONARD: No need to fear, Nicola is here. I have a note here, what do DJs really do while they're playing records? That's a good question. I hate to tell you. Some read the papers, some play the stock-market, call up their stock-brokers between records – that's true, folks – some call up their lady friends, and some just play with their stylus. (*Smiles.*) And some long to scream obscenities over the air! The mad DJ. And they all use words so sumptuously for your pleasure. Do you ever listen to your words, Brazil? Never, thank goodness, but never mind. Everybody needs us, after all – (*Lightly.*) – we're the new jokers of the pack, we're the new clowns, we tell it how it should be. And we're going to lick the blues. Each week I try to lick the blues – this time with a flysprayer, I have it out, I'm spraying it, I'm spraying them now, they're falling to the ground, curling up black and dead, legs in the air – we've done it. Don't spit on the animals. We're going to make it aren't we, get through to the other side, of course we are – and if you've just seen some horrible things, on the television, bomb blasts, unemployment, politicians, and all that part of our good old England, and you've switched it off to listen to me, sensibly! Then remember, no need to fear, we're going to lick it, so Shout it out! Things can only get better and better – so Shout it out! We have the greatest day of the century tomorrow, so there's something to look forward to, so let's Shout it out! Yes, you, madam, get out of the bath, and *Shout it out!* And you, love, take your hands away from here and Shout it out!

Throw that away, lad, and SHOUT IT OUT! Come on Grandad, SHOUT IT OUT! You too, Nicola Davies, SHOUT IT OUT! Let's have some real music. I said SHOUT IT OUT! LOUDER! I can't hear you, don't spit on the animals – this is nineteen hundred and seventy eight, this is Len Brazil – this is Crazy Competition Week – be there tomorrow – and once more SHOUT IT OUT!

Music stops after crescendo. REX *has entered, stares at* LEONARD. *Total silence, long pause.*

LEONARD: Shit. I wasn't going to do that.

He flicks a switch. A record comes on, incredibly loud. The lights fade.

End of Act One.

ACT TWO

In the blackout we hear two girls' voices singing 'I Can Give You Love' – one of the Yellow Jacks' songs (the words and music appear at the end of the play). They sing the whole of the first verse loudly and slightly harshly to a piano accompaniment, woodenly played.

Scene One

NICOLA*'s bedroom. Saturday lunchtime.* NICOLA *sitting on the bed, brushing her hair.* SUSAN *moving round the room, munching some cheese puffs. A packet with one sandwich in it is on the dressing table.*

SUSAN: You ought to eat something.

NICOLA: I don't need to. Not hungry.

SUSAN (*turning away*): You won't do very well if you don't eat. Here.

She tosses NICOLA *some cheese puffs.* NICOLA *doesn't bother to catch them.*

NICOLA: No don't want anything. (*Smiles.*) Good sort of diet, this competition, I lost a lot. See – it's come off. (*She feels her waist.*)

SUSAN: You don't need to lose any. (*Pause.*) You're getting skinny. (*Pause.*) You look a bit pale, you know.

NICOLA: I want to look pale.

SUSAN: They coming for you in a car?

NICOLA: No, I'm going there.

SUSAN (*turning round the room*): They can't even be bothered to fetch you. Not much left in your room, is there. (*Smiles.*) All this has sort of cleaned it out, hasn't it. I mean the competition . . .

52

NICOLA: Yes, I put most of it in, didn't I. It all came in useful.

SUSAN (*to herself*): Anyway, there's the concert tonight. (*Smiling, looking at her.*) Is that the lipstick I bought with you – it made my lips so sore, and they itched like anything. (*She rubs her lip.*) Still itch all the time, if I think about them. I want to get some white lipstick. I'm growing old, do you know that? (*She looks at* NICOLA.) Yes! How do you feel then . . . about it?

NICOLA: O.K. . . . Fine . . . (*Quiet.*) I'm going to be all right. I've been preparing for it. Sat here by the record player all night, listening to records all night, really quietly so *no-one* could hear me.

SUSAN (*very lightly*): It'd be more exciting, wouldn't it really, if you were going to be shot if you lost, or something like that. I mean, then you really would be nervous. If they were going to put you in the electric chair, tie you up in a black chair, and press the button, and – (*Smiles.*) – instead they'll just give you a consolation prize if you lose . . . that's not very exciting, is it? (*She picks up the packet of cheese puffs.*) You're very lucky anyway – you could be going to London. Never been out of this town have you?

NICOLA: Not really, hardly.

SUSAN: And you've already won that LP –

NICOLA: They haven't sent it yet.

SUSAN (*excited*): Going with them to London, Nicola, you can't do much better than that.

NICOLA: Well I've got into there anyway – into the radio building. (*Slight smile.*) I'm going there.

SUSAN: If you go with them – You'll have to be careful of the heavies – they'll still have their heavies with them, they go everywhere with them . . . when they were playing in Coventry in March or whenever it was, and I went, you know . . . and you know what happened, somebody I saw . . . she was throwing herself down on the carpet the whole time at the exit, after the concert, and when they picked her up, she just threw herself down again, and they got angry, the heavies did, so they kicked her – not that hard – they kicked her, *one* did, and so anyway, after a bit, she got up, and went and lay down somewhere else . . . and she made herself sick or something on the floor, in a pool . . . so this heavy, he wasn't one of the biggest, but he came over to her . . . and he said something, I couldn't hear it, and she didn't move, so he got her by the hair, not very hard, but he got by the hair and rubbed her face in it, like that. I saw it. Gave her a quick rub – (*She demonstrates with the head of a teddy-bear by the bed.*) – just once – to stop her doing it.

NICOLA: You've told me before. That's not going to happen to me.

SUSAN (*fast*): I didn't tell you . . . didn't tell you this. That same time, by the place, I was walking along, and I saw this policeman, he wasn't very old for a policeman, he can't have been that old, he was standing in a doorway, I saw him, he was all by himself and he was swearing his head off, he was, with his teeth kind of clenched. And he had water in his eyes, he was crying, well I don't know if he was really crying but his face was all screwed up and red, and really vicious looking, and there was stuff coming out of his eyes. Down his face. He wasn't old. I saw him anyway, it's true. I remember it more than anything else.

The phone rings. NICOLA *moves out of bedroom area*

to the phone. She picks it up and answers it.

NICOLA: Yes . . .

REX'S VOICE (*on the phone, very soft, we hardly hear it*): Nicola, Nicola Davies?

NICOLA: Yes.

LEONARD'S VOICE (*on the phone, very suddenly*): Hello there, Nicola, this is Leonard here, sorry to drop in like this, we're on the air, love – (*Funny voice*) – in front of the listening thousands, at this moment. I've just been talking to your fine opponent, Jane, and I wanted to know love, are you OK . . . ?

SUSAN (*shouts*): What's he ringing you up again for?

NICOLA: Yes – I'm very well thank you.

LEONARD: Getting a good lunch, are you – what have you had?

NICOLA: For lunch – some water.

LEONARD: Some water – is that all?

NICOLA: Yes. I'm fine thank you.

LEONARD: You must have something else, Nicola, to get really ready for it.

NICOLA: Yes, Leonard.

LEONARD: The reason I've called, love, is so that we both can tell all the people listening that DON'T FORGET, it's the Competition of the Century today.

NICOLA: Yes.

LEONARD: And don't *you* forget that you're having your photograph taken.

NICOLA: No I won't Leonard.

LEONARD (*slight pause*): OK love . . . we'll be seeing each other very soon, so till then, 'bye, love.

NICOLA (*quiet*): Goodbye. (*She puts down the receiver.*)

SUSAN: Can't leave you alone, can he?

NICOLA: No . . . that's good, isn't it. I think he likes me. I'm going to meet him. (*Smiles.*) I am.

SUSAN: Yes, you really are, aren't you, Leonard Brazil. Do your Mum and Dad know about this . . . ?

NICOLA: They've gone out. I told them – don't think they believed me, or they didn't hear properly – *Mum* would have listened to the programme – but they might have got excited – but they don't like me doing that much.

SUSAN (*hardly listening*): You wearing just that . . . ?

NICOLA: Yes.

SUSAN: You should put this on. (*She pulls out another dress.*) You want to look a bit sexy don't you . . . get him excited . . .

NICOLA: This is OK.

SUSAN: He'll probably give you a bit of a squeeze, quick squeeze at your tits.

NICOLA: No he won't – don't be stupid.

SUSAN: You know what to do don't you, tell him you're deaf in one ear.

NICOLA: Why?

SUSAN: So you can ask for every question to be said twice. Also it'll get him on your side, won't it? You got to try everything you can think of to win. And you'll have to be really on the lookout won't you – he'll try to put you through a lot for something as big as that – he's not going to give something like that away easily, is he? – come on, I'll do that. (*She snatches the hairbrush, begins to brush* NICOLA's *hair.*) He'll probably hold up pictures of Ross in the nude, to put you off, you ought to put spikes on your shoes – so you can kick him under the table – that's what you've got to do – give 'em their money's worth!

NICOLA (*quiet, determined*): I'm going to win, you know.

56

SUSAN: Yes; well if the other one wins we'll really do her won't we? We'll finish her. (*She moves away.*)

NICOLA (*sharp*): Why don't you ever keep still?

SUSAN: Because I don't.

NICOLA: You're always doing that. (*Nervous.*) Please . . .

SUSAN: Why shouldn't I? What's the point of keeping still – I've never kept still *ever* – (*Moving up to* NICOLA.) Come on, you're going to eat something now. (*She picks up the sandwich.*) Come on.

> NICOLA *doesn't take it.*

SUSAN (*suddenly very loud*): Come on, YOU GOT TO EAT! YOU MUST! Now open your gob. (*She pushes the sandwich into* NICOLA*'s mouth.*) I might come to London with you, you know – if you ever get there. Which you probably won't.

NICOLA (*chewing*): You going to be listening?

SUSAN (slight smile): I expect so. You ought to stay in London, don't you think . . . if you get there. We both ought to. Yes. Get out of here! (*She pushes the sandwich into* NICOLA*'s mouth.*) Come on – eat it all, get it down. Swallow it, Nicola. (*Loud.*) YOU GOT TO! RIGHT DOWN.

> *Long pause.* NICOLA *swallows.*

SUSAN: Now you're ready.

Blackout.

Scene Two

The studio. BIG JOHN *sitting.* LEONARD BRAZIL *standing.* MICK *sweeping up the studio.*

LEONARD (*moving about, speaking to* REX, *who isn't there*): I want these seats adjusted . . . could I please have these seats adjusted . . . Where is he . . . (*He swings round.*) And if that phone rings once more I will have it decapitated. (*Slight pause.*) It's that oily sod Johnson, he –

The phone rings. LEONARD *picks it up fast. We hear a slimy nasal voice speaking fast on the other end. We catch a few words . . .*

VOICE: Leonard . . . a few words again . . . congratulations . . . just want to remind you . . . Studio A . . . security . . .

As he speaks, LEONARD's *replies are brusque.*

LEONARD (*on the phone*): Yes . . . yes . . . yes . . . Quite . . . Yes . . . All right . . . (*Louder.*) OK . . .Fine! (*He slams down the phone.*) Keeps congratulating me on how things are going. That one was to tell me the precise arrangements for Ross's visit to this building – and not to forget to plug the rest of their tour – and remember you're carrying a bumper lot of commercials –

JOHN (*smiling*): It's going very well isn't it. I haven't seen anything like this for a long time. I like this atmosphere tremendously.

LEONARD (*by the coffee machine*): Yes. (*Quiet, looking at the machine.*) Do you think if one kicked this machine it'd start playing music?

JOHN: Is what I hear true?

LEONARD (*taking his coffee from the machine*): What do you hear, John?

JOHN: That you've been made an offer – that you-know-who have made a whopping big offer –

LEONARD (*matter-of-fact*): Yes. (*Pause.*) It appears I have been offered the job –

JOHN (*smiling*): What? You really have. Congratulations! That's wonderful news isn't it! (*Smiles.*) The station must be really pleased – when you've just started making us a profit. (REX *enters.*) Have you heard? He's been made a firm offer!

REX (*smiles*): He hasn't! Have you, Leonard?

LEONARD (*matter-of-fact*): Nice, isn't it?

MICK: Er – can I just say Mr Brazil how pleased I am that . . . I mean can I congratulate you . . . I mean . . . It's really great isn't it – really great, you'll show them in London.

LEONARD: Yes Mick.

MICK: They won't have seen anything like it, you must be feeling great now, I would be.

LEONARD: That's right Mick thank you. (MICK *grins nervously and leaves.*)

JOHN: When do you take up residence – after this holiday?

LEONARD (*smiling*): I'm not sure, John, that I'm going at all.

REX: What?

JOHN: What do you mean, you don't know?

LEONARD (*smiles*): We'll be seeing about that.

JOHN: Well there's a lot of money there, and the size of the audience – you'll be playing to an audience of millions – you've always been good at that.

LEONARD (*smiling at him, his manner dangerously light*): That's right . . . that's very true John . . .

REX *moves around the studio, getting ready.*

LEONARD (*fast to* JOHN): I think we should put some music behind you today – don't you? Behind the News. A

59

french horn perhaps, sounding your approach – so you
seem to gallop in here on horseback, and a banjo under
you for lighter parts –

JOHN: Don't think we quite need that . . .

LEONARD: You were a good idea of mine, you know, John.

JOHN (*slight smile*): Of course I was.

LEONARD: My stroke of genius – saying we must have live
news and not network.

JOHN (*to* REX, *as he tidies*): It's the best thing that's ever
happened to me – I'd been cut back, one of the many to
be lopped off the paper; I was lucky.

LEONARD (*laughs*): and I've never been able to take the
news seriously since. Like most newsreaders, of course,
you have no idea what you're saying – when you read it
out. Have you?

JOHN: Of course I do.

LEONARD (*loud*): Rubbish. Last week, I wrote items of total
schoolboy gibberish – announcing that the Third World
War had just broken out and was due to arrive in five
minutes and that the entire Royal family had contracted
rabies – and I asked the girl downstairs – Carol – to slip
them in. You came in here, sat down, and read them
straight out without a blink. (*Grins.*) Without any
comment. (*American voice.*) You're highly dangerous,
John.

JOHN (*startled*): You didn't do that . . . ? When was that?
You had me for a moment. (*Smiles to* REX.) He can take
in anybody really if he wants to. (*Smiles.*) This man's
rather good, you know . . . he's rather good.

REX: Yes, of course. (*He has collected a tray covered in
letters and small parcels wrapped in coloured paper.*)
Here's two letters for you. (*He drops them in front of*
LEONARD.) And all these presents and good luck cards

have come in for the two girls. They've been pouring in all the time before they were even chosen. Some are from old age pensioners, shows how wide our audience is, and some are really aggressive and jealous ones from other kids.

LEONARD (*glancing briefly at his own letters*): Make sure they get one letter each – a pleasant one, Rex. And get this place tidy – we're going to have guests.

REX (*not moving*): Look at that, he hardly glances at his letters. His mother could have died for all we know, or his lady friends could have started eating each other – (*To* BIG JOHN.) – a different one each week – and he'd never show anything.

LEONARD (*putting letter away*): Yes.

REX: And have you heard about his flat? It is totally bare, almost, except for hundred of books.

JOHN: Yes, I know.

REX: And you know he's hardly eaten all week – so I hear. Gone off his food.

JOHN: The nervous strain – with his offer hanging over him. (*Smiles.*) I hope you're going to give us a great show, Leonard – for all the family.

REX: Of course he is.

JOHN: It's a specially cold day, freezing, out there. Wonderful, isn't it? Everybody'll be indoors, you've got them sitting there already. Probably going to get the biggest audiences we've ever had.

LEONARD (*looking up*): Well, Rex is not going on the air today, is he? He's not going near a microphone.

REX: What?

LEONARD (*lightly*): He's having no part of this competition.

REX (*startled*): What do you mean by that? (*Getting excited.*) What on earth . . .

61

LEONARD: You're not going on the air, that's what I mean. You've been fired.

REX: What? You didn't mean that, did you? But I've been working things out for it . . . What do you mean. (*Working himself up.*) I've worked all week on this competition – I have, haven't I?

LEONARD (*matter-of-fact*): I think you'd better leave us alone, John, the boy's getting excited. Go on, go and find some really juicy news. (*Slight smile.*) Must have something good, mustn't we?

JOHN (*getting up*): And what if there isn't any?

LEONARD: Use your imagination, of course. Write some.

REX (*as soon as* JOHN *has gone*): What do you mean I can't do anything?

LEONARD: You can't . . . I've decided.

REX: But I must, don't you see . . . I . . .

LEONARD (*dryly*): No. It's not good for you, is it?

REX: What do you mean it's not good for me? (*Loud.*) Why have you decided to do this?

LEONARD: I've told you.

REX: I mean when everything's going so well for you. (*Loud.*) Why?

LEONARD: I don't think you should be let loose, Rex. So I've fired you.

REX: You don't really mean that, do you? Do you? (*No reply; he changes tone.*) Look, please, Leonard, *please*. I've prepared something specially. I have. Just for today please. I've been waiting all week for this. (*Loud.*) I am *asking* you, Leonard. I've worked well for you, haven't I? HAVEN'T I?

LEONARD (*smiles*): You're not going on the air, Rex, and that's final. You're going to run things more efficiently than you've ever done before – for the last time. And you're not going to make a single mistake. Go on.

REX (*doesn't move*): No.

>   LEONARD *looks up.*

REX: I've got to do something.

LEONARD (*looks at him*): Why have you got to?

REX: Because I want to – (*Matter-of-fact.*) Because I'm determined to. (*Pause.*)

LEONARD: You're determined, are you?

REX: Yes, Leonard.

LEONARD (*matter-of-fact*): You worry me, you know, Rex.

REX (*quiet*): Do I?

LEONARD: You can have just one minute. Sixty seconds. I shouldn't let you, of course – you're still fired. You're leaving after the competition.

REX: Thanks. Thank you, Leonard.

LEONARD: I should keep your thanks till afterwards. You've got a job to do, do it. (REX *is moving off.*) You know this equipment is about to expire don't you. When it gets hot, it smells really tired – probably give out today.

REX: It'll last. It doesn't matter what it looks like.

LEONARD: One wouldn't want to do an operation with rusty instruments would one? (*He looks at the equipment.*) This is all really tawdry.

>   REX *comes back in quickly.*

REX: There's one of them out there.

LEONARD: One of them?

REX: One of the girls.

LEONARD: Well bring her in of course. Don't let her wait out there.

>   REX *goes out.*

63

LEONARD (*matter-of-fact*): Better see what we've netted, hadn't we.

REX (*coming back with* NICOLA): Here.

LEONARD: Hello. (*Pause.*) Which one are you?

REX: Nicola.

LEONARD (*gently*): Let her speak for herself.

NICOLA: Nicola Davies.

LEONARD: Nicola Davies. (*Pause.*) I . . . thought you'd look a little different . . .

NICOLA (*embarrassed*): Oh . . . Did you?

LEONARD: Do I look different?

NICOLA: No – not really.

LEONARD: So you're in the studio now. (*To* REX.) Have they checked her downstairs?

REX: I don't think so – she just wandered in – after they'd done the photo outside.

LEONARD: You better do it. (*To* NICOLA, *gently*.) I'm afraid it's ridiculous, but everybody that comes up here has to be submitted, that's what they call it, to a bomb check. I'm sorry . . . it ought to have been done downstairs.

NICOLA: Oh . . . yes. I didn't know.

She opens her bag.

LEONARD: Rex'll do the honours. (*As* REX *searches her.*) We get hoaxes all the time – twice as much at night. Last week somebody phones in to say there was a purple bomb, whatever that meant. (*To* REX.) That's OK. Thank you. (*He smiles at* NICOLA.) You like to sit down – careful where you sit . . . Do you want anything to eat? We'll try to get you anything you like.

REX *crosses over to the box.*

NICOLA: No thank you.

LEONARD: We're nearly ready for you. (*He puts his headphones on;* REX *is in the box*.) OK, *stand by*. Where's the other one? (*He presses a putton. There is a roar of music, really loud.* NICOLA *starts.* LEONARD *fades the music down. To* NICOLA.) Don't worry, nothing in the world to worry about. (*The music fades down; the red light goes on. Into mike*.) Stop where you are! Don't switch off! For I, LB, am here. This is Crazy Competition Week. This is the final programme – how are you all? On this savage cold day . . . it's warm up here, though. So this is the Big One. For me, too. We've all got to it, and we're going straight into it, folks. (*Slight accent*.) Get the bleeder over and wrapped up. Both girls are smiling, just a little bit tense; we'll be meeting them in a moment. Right now, let's hear one of the prizes in full flow – and he'll lead us into a few bubbling commercials –

ROSS's VOICE (*on tape*): The things I don't like – that's a difficult one. I like most things.

LEONARD (*cutting off the tape. Looking at her*): Know that voice?

NICOLA: Yes – it's Ross's voice.

LEONARD: Rex – we're minus one girl. (*He smiles, flicks a switch*.)

ROSS's VOICE: I don't like violence – of any sort, of course, or people that provoke it, create it, you know, exploit it, they're criminals really, aren't they?

LEONARD (*switching it off*): He's in fine form, isn't he?

NICOLA: Yes.

LEONARD (*calm, smiling*): They're waiting for the Competition of the Century down there – (*Looking at* NICOLA.) – and we may not be able to give it to them. (*He flicks the switch on again*.)

ROSS's VOICE: I mean *we* don't use violence – I know people, some morons and journalists, have said so, but everybody just has a party when we play.

LEONARD: Got a good voice, hasn't he?

NICOLA: Yes.

ROSS's VOICE (*in the background as they talk*): And I don't like parasites, journalists, reporters, people that criticise.

LEONARD (*calm, smiling*): Rex – come here.

REX *immediately comes down from the box.*

ROSS's VOICE (*as* REX *comes down*): And write malicious things about people . . . and also I don't like people that get above themselves.

LEONARD *switches him off.*

LEONARD: I was thinking, we'd better give them something to drink, something a little strong, so they don't worry.

REX: That's a good idea.

LEONARD: Go and arrange it. (REX *moves.* LEONARD *still very calm.*) And you'd better find the other one, hadn't you, wherever she is, we need her in one minute –

REX (*smiles*): Right, Leonard. (*He goes.*)

LEONARD (*to* NICOLA): You OK?

NICOLA (*quiet*): Yes.

LEONARD *flicks the switch again.*

ROSS's VOICE: I'm not a prude – Christ, you've only got to ask Ken or Dave, or any of my friends, but I really don't like sex where it doesn't belong, I mean –

LEONARD *switches it off.*

LEONARD (*matter-of-fact*): You better come and sit over

here love . . . please. Plenty of time, there's nothing to worry about. (NICOLA *moves over to the chair by the microphone.*) Looking forward to it? (*Pause.*) Are you?

NICOLA: Yes . . . I am.

LEONARD (*as* NICOLA *crosses*): Good. Don't suppose you ever thought you'd get here.

NICOLA: No – I sort of hoped –

LEONARD: And you are. You're here. (*Quiet.*) This is the big one, Nicola. You want to listen to him, do you? (*He flicks on the switch as he settles* NICOLA *into the chair, adjusts its height, tests its distance from microphone.*) Are you comfortable?

NICOLA *nods; as this happens,* LEONARD *stares at her,* ROSS'*s voice booms loud from the speakers in background.*

ROSS'S VOICE: I mean I agree with that too, and I don't like women who swear. I like them to be – I know this is corny – I like them to be feminine, I'm afraid so, and . . . I know this list's getting kind of long, but you know one thing I really don't like is dirty cutlery. I mean it happens in England, it's much better in the States, but you book in to a really good hotel, and you wake up in the morning for your breakfast, and the first thing you see is dirty cutlery, really filthy cutlery, I mean people don't work in this country, I mean that's the trouble really, isn't it, and somebody really has got to do something . . . I like cheerful music.

LEONARD *switches him off as* REX *enters.*

REX: She's here.

JANE *enters.*

REX: And she's been checked.

LEONARD: Hello, I'm Leonard – cut it fine, didn't you?

JANE: I'm sorry. I couldn't find it. I am sorry – it's not easy to find.

LEONARD: It's OK, love, you're here now. We're ready to go. (*To* REX.) Have you got the drink?

REX: Yes I have. (*He produces a bottle, moves to get glasses.*)

LEONARD: Come and sit here – do you want a drink?

JANE: I don't know.

LEONARD (*pours some out*): Come on, have some, it won't bite you.

    NICOLA *drinks.*

REX: Jane doesn't want any.

LEONARD (*jocular*): Don't know why we don't give them vitamin injections as well. Nothing to worry about, girls, I'm just going to ask you a few questions, don't worry about anything I might do, I'm not going to sit here, I may roam about . . .

REX (*producing roses from a tray on the side*): I thought they'd like a rose each – a present from Leicester Sound – two white roses make them look nice –

LEONARD (*lightly*): They look nice anyway – don't you. Do you want to wear them? Rex's little gift.

    JANE *nods*; REX *pins a rose on her*; LEONARD *hands a rose to* NICOLA.

LEONARD (*to* REX, *referring to* JANE): She needs to be a little higher –

REX: Yes . . . That was a low-key start.

LEONARD: Of course – this is a family show. (*He puts on his headphones.*) OK, that's enough, stop fiddling with her –

(REX *stops fiddling with* JANE *and returns to his box.* LEONARD *smiles. To* GIRLS.) Now don't worry, nobody's going to get hurt, are they? (*Flicks switch.*) Before the commercials that was the one and only Ross, who'll be entering this building very soon. We have the two lucky and lovely girls with me – Hello Nicola.

NICOLA: Hello.

LEONARD: And now Jane – who's looking very composed . . . Rex has just given them a couple of roses – one of course white, the other is red – we have a real War of the Roses coming up here. I wish you could smell them, breathe into the mikes, girls. (JANE *leans forward, he restrains her.*) Here come the questions, glistening on a silver tray. (*He picks up some white cards from desk.*) Thank you, Rex.

REX (*loud, excited, important*): We've got one of the biggest audiences we've ever had – it's a great sight. The studio's looking very fine. The competitors are in perfect condition, sleek and healthy, and there's traffic jams for miles –

LEONARD: Enough of this gibber! You're going to make some noises, aren't you?

REX: I am indeed Leonard – I'm going to make this noise for a right answer . . . (*Loud bell.*)

LEONARD: That's a nice noise for a right answer.

REX: And this noise for a wrong answer . . . (*Loud vicious buzzing noise.*)

LEONARD: That's a grisly noise for a wrong answer.

REX: And I'll be making this noise for 'Don't Knows' . . . (*Funny, irritating noise.*)

LEONARD: Yes, girls – *No* 'Don't knows' – have a guess. If you say, 'Don't know', – (REX *makes the 'Don't Know' noise.*) you lose a life; if you lose three lives, you're out

69

of the game, and if it's a tie –

REX: If it's a tie –

LEONARD (*quiet*): We want *you* to vote, ladies and gentlemen, for who put up the best show – so keep your ears skinned, or peeled, or however you like your ears done.

REX: Where are the other questions, Leonard?

LEONARD: In my head, Rex.

REX: And –

LEONARD (*cutting him off suddenly*): And this now – this here – is – The Competition of the Century. (*Quiet, matter-of-fact.*) Jane and Nicola are the contestants; I, Len Brazil, am putting the questions. (*Quiet.*) 5, 4, 3, 2, 1, ZERO! And the very first question is for Jane . . . And the question is: Jane – (*Quick.*) – How old is Ken?

JANE: Ken? He's . . . twenty-one.

Bell rings loudly.

LEONARD: Correct! The lady is correct. Do you know how many months?

NICOLA (*fast*): Six.

LEONARD: It's Jane's question, Nicola.

JANE: Six months.

Bell rings again.

LEONARD: One point to Jane. (*Suddenly loud.*) Jane has one point! (LEONARD's *manner begins to quicken, his DJ instinct coming out despite himself.* LEONARD's *highly charged inner state during the competition should be underlined by his constant movement away from his chair and his total absorption in* NICOLA *to the exclusion of* JANE. *He stares at* NICOLA, *touches her chair, stands over her during her long speech.*) And the first question for

Nicola is – the question in Round One for Nicola is, and she's looking very calm . . . is – What is Dave's favourite food – and when does he like to eat it?

NICOLA: Dave's favourite food . . . it's fresh . . . it's home-made bread, and he likes it in the morning – (*Silence, nervous.*) – at sunrise, I think.

Bell rings loudly.

LEONARD (*staring at* NICOLA): That's correct, Nicola. That's the answer that was wanted. You're doing fine, Nicola. So is Jane, both of you are doing fine. (*He has got up, is moving around past his mike.*) Round Two of the Competition of the Century. Another Nicola question . . . Tell me, Nicola, which famous historical and Shakespearean character is traditionally associated with Leicester?

NICOLA: What? (*Pause.*) I . . .

LEONARD: A famous character by Will Shakespeare, associated with this fine city of ours. Have to hurry you –

NICOLA: I'm sorry . . . I . . . I don't know.

Very loud buzz.

LEONARD: You musn't say that, Nicola, I'm afraid . . . it's not allowed. So you have to lose a life, don't you. (*'Competition' voice.*) Nicola has lost a life. Do *you* know Jane?

JANE (*about to reply, then decides not to*): I . . . I . . . (*She shakes her head.*)

LEONARD: Careful . . . NO 'Don't knows'. (*'Competition' voice.*) Neither of the girls know. Which is a surprise! The answer is King Lear – the man with the long beard. (*He moves, picks up the next question. Loud.*) And now Jane, what is the name of the new office block near the

71

prison?

JANE: That . . . it's called . . . I think it's called The New Walk Centre.

Bell rings.

LEONARD: Correct. She has given a right answer. Well up on this fine city of ours, aren't you. Good. (*Funny voice.*) It's completely changed since I was a lad here. It's been torn up and re-planted. You've got two points now, Jane. You're doing well. You're both doing well. Here's another question for you, Nicola Davies – wait for it – when was the Haymarket Centre opened? – Nicola – the great Haymarket Centre. What was the year when its full glory was seen?

NICOLA: I . . . I . . . (*She bites her lip.*) Was it about ten years ago?

Loud 'Wrong answer' noise, repeated twice.

LEONARD: That's the wrong answer, I'm afraid, Nicola. It wasn't ten years ago, no.

NICOLA: Sorry, I – I don't know these sort of questions.

LEONARD: You musn't say that, Nicola – must have a go, got to have a go at everything – the atmosphere beginning to get a little tense here – not to worry. Nothing to worry about. The year was – (*Loud.*) – 1971. Of course. And our great thanks to Alderman Townshend for setting those questions. There are a lot more I may use later. The score is three points to Jane, and Nicolas Davies is trailing behind with one point. Round Three now folks, of the Competition – which is carrying the greatest prize we have ever offered. My questions start here, girls, this is the first one. I'm going to say some words now . . . rather fast. I want you to tell me six of them. Ready Nicola. I'm going to say them very very fast, so be on the look-out. (*He fires the words out sharply.*) Killer, Bottle, Junk, Rifle, Tune, Cheeseburger, Sickroom, Commercial, Knife, Disaster, Stereo, Limousine, Tube, Scar, Women's Lib, Cash Quickie, Needle, Platform, Pill, Dungaree, Snowball, Lump, Oil, Rape, Fire, Neddy, Assassin, Cardboard, Vegetable. (*Pause.*)

NICOLA: Assassin . . . Bottle . . . Needle . . . (*Pause, she begins to panic.*)

LEONARD: That's only three, Nicola . . . Three.

NICOLA (*biting her lip*): Oil . . . Pill . . .

LEONARD: Have to hurry you now . . . Something you ought to know about, being a woman.

NICOLA (*pause*): Women's Lib.

  Bell rings loudly.

LEONARD: Well done Nicola – well done. You now have two whole points, yes you do. (*He turns to* JANE.) You thought I was going to do the same to you, Jane, didn't you?

JANE: Yes.

LEONARD: But I'm not! (*Fast.*) Yes I am. Six please of the following. (*Very fast, even louder.*) Chocolate, Wire, Ratings, Tank, Plastic, Movie, Goldfish, Shares, Black, Judge, Union, Red Grass, Steel, Sniper, Index, Trash, Hit, Disco, Chart-climber, Bomb, Cell, Beans, Hook, Barrier, Kite, TV, Kennel, Motorway.

  Silence. JANE *stares at him.*

LEONARD: Six please, Jane, quickly –

JANE: Chocolate . . . Motorway. (*Silence. She panics, head in hands.*)

LEONARD: Quick Jane, I have to hurry you, I'm afraid. (*Pause.*) You're running out of time.

JANE (*panicking*): I don't know.

Very loud 'Don't know' piercing noise.

LEONARD: I'm afraid you lose a life too, Jane. (*'Competition' voice.*) Jane loses a life! Both have lost a life now. Neck-and-neck. That's OK, nothing to worry about. Doing very well, Jane. (*He stares at* NICOLA.) Nicola is sitting very still. This is the Competition of the Century. What I want you to do now Jane, is, in your own words, talk about a subject I will give you for *one whole* minute. And the subject is – Jane is smiling, she's straining at the leash – and the subject is . . . folks . . . 'Why do I want to go to London', if indeed you do. It is of course just one of the prizes of this Competition. From now!

Silence.

JANE: I . . . I . . . want to go there . . . to London because I've always . . . (*She stops.*) Are you, are you allowed to repeat things, words?

LEONARD: Yes. You're allowed that. Come on.

JANE: Because, because, I've always wanted to go there . . . and there's a shop in a street, I don't know which street, I saw it . . . this shop, late at night . . . when I was there once, in London, it's the only time I've ever been, and it was open at that time, I mean when shops aren't open, really, and so I wanted to go there, it had big posters in it, very very big posters, some of pop stars, some of politicians, and things, and one of a very fat woman with no clothes on . . . and it had flags all round, the shop did, I mean, and pictures, and names of streets, and souvenirs, cigarettes, and everything. And there was

music coming out of it, very loud . . . right out into the
street . . . be good to go and shop there. And I mean to
go and see things, that you know are famous, always
been told about, and buy clothes, and look if you can't
buy, because there are clothes shops everywhere, not
like anywhere else, and see everything, all the night life
. . . and I want –

   Bell goes.

LEONARD: Well done Jane, thank you for that. That was
   very well done, wasn't it? Very good Jane, Excellent. I'll
   give you three out of five for that. So now Jane has six
   whole points all to herself. 'Six – points – Jane!' And
   now Nicola Davies, the subject for you is – (*Pause. He
   stares at her.*)

NICOLA: Yes?

LEONARD: The subject on which you've got to talk for not
   less and not more than one minute is – wait for it –
   (*Loud.*) – the last pop concert you went to. (*Pause.*)

NICOLA: The last . . . the last pop concert I went to . . . it
   was here in Leicester – (*She swallows.*) – and Ross and
   the group were playing, and I queued to get in for a long
   time . . .

LEONARD: How long? How long did you queue for, Nicola?

NICOLA (*completely thrown by his interruption*): I . . .

LEONARD (*staring at her, quieter but matter-of-fact*): How
   long did you queue for, love?

NICOLA: I don't know, not . . .

   'Don't know' noise, very loud.

LEONARD: No sorry. We don't count that! Rex is a little
   trigger-happy, watching out for 'Don't knows'. Come on
   Nicola.

NICOLA: We queued for a day and a night, I think . . . it was a bit wet . . . you see, and the stone, the pavement, was very hard and cold, much harder than you think – because we slept there you see . . . it was all right and . . . and then a man came up, it was late you know then, dark and everything, and he'd come to sell us hot dogs and things, he came out there and he set up along the side of the queue, it was a very long queue, and then soon another . . . another came up out of the dark, and then there was another one, till there were lots and lots all along the line, really close. (*She looks up.*)

LEONARD (*staring at her, very close*): Go on Nicola! Keep going. You're doing fine. You've got to keep going.

NICOLA: Oh! I thought it was enough.

LEONARD: I'm afraid it's not.

NICOLA: Oh . . . and . . . (*Lost for words, she is extremely nervous.*) – and then we went inside . . . and the concert . . . and it was them of course, and it was, you know . . . well it was all squashed – and some people rushed up and fought to get close – and there was a bit of biting, and that sort of thing, when they called out to us; they seemed a long way off – a very long way away, in their yellow and everything. They weren't loud – but they made you feel – I felt something come up, you know, a little sort of . . . (*A second of slight clenched feeling.*) I got, you know, a bit worked up inside . . . they were moving very slowly on stage like they'd been slowed down, made me feel strange – then they held things up, waved it at us, smiling and everything. they waved yellow scarves. Ross had a bit of yellow string he waved, I think it was, a bit of yellow rope, and I half wanted to kick the girl in front of me or something because I couldn't see; all the way through I had to look at her great back, pressed right up against it. I remember I half wanted to *get at it*. Move it. And I nearly dropped a ring. (*She pulls at her finger.*) I'd been pulling at, put it on specially. (*Very nervous, she smiles.*) If you drop anything it's gone for ever you know – can't bend down if you're standing – (*Smiles.*) – and if you drop yourself . . . then you'd be gone. When you rush out at the end, you can see all the millions of things that have been dropped shining all over the floor, nobody gets a chance to pick them up. And then it was finished – you know, the concert, and I came outside. It was cold, I was feeling a bit funny. Just walked along out there and I thought maybe I was bleeding. I looked but I wasn't. Some people like to be after a concert . . . but I wasn't.

Pause. Bell rings.

LEONARD: Well done Nicola! That was very very nice. Fabulous, wasn't it folks, fabulous. I'll give you five whole points for that. The very most I'm empowered to give. You now have seven whole points. Now what we want you to do is to sing a song, one of the Yellow Jacks' songs, and you must try not to get any of the words wrong. Rex knows the words, and he'll be watching . . .

NICOLA *gets down off her chair, moves away.*

LEONARD (*sharp, still his DJ voice*): Where are you going, Nicola . . .

NICOLA *half turns.* LEONARD *presses a button; covering music bursts out, the volume then dips.*

LEONARD (*louder*): Where are you going?
NICOLA (*turns, faces him*): I was . . .

Pause. Music playing.

LEONARD: Where on earth do you think you're going?

NICOLA: I . . . I wanted a glass of water.

LEONARD (*calm*): You don't walk away like that, do you – you can't leave the room, Nicola – we're in the middle of a competition, don't you realise –

NICOLA: I know.

LEONARD: You've got to stay here, till we finish. (*He stares at her.*) Haven't you . . . (*She doesn't move.*) Haven't you?

NICOLA: Yes, I . . . just wanted for a moment –

LEONARD: Come back here. We're on the air. Rex will get something afterwards. (*He flicks the switch, the music dies.*) We're here, never fear. Nicola's just had a little accident, went for a walkabout – (*'Competition' voice.*) in the MIDDLE of the Competition of the Century! Extraordinary, but she's back now. The question is, Nicola, Nicola, now sing a song, and the song is 'Yellow Blues'. Stand up Nicola will you; Nicola is standing up, and remember the words must be right.

NICOLA: Yes.

Pause. She is standing, begins to sing, almost finishes a verse,* then very loud 'Wrong Answer' noise.

LEONARD: You've gone wrong, I'm afraid, Nicola. No points. Jane now, it's your turn. Your song is 'I can give you love' by the Yellow Jacks. Like to stand up for it? Jane is standing up now! (*Fast.*) Rex is sweating, we're all sweating, the girls have been chewing our fingers down to the bone. Ready Jane.

* Words and music at end of play.

JANE *begins to sing*; very quiet. It lasts longer than* NICOLA*'s; eventually the 'Wrong answer' buzzer goes.*

LEONARD: Jane, you're wrong this time, I'm afraid. No score for that round at all. But I think I'm going to give her a point, because she lasted quite a long time. Well done Jane. The girls have nice voices, don't they, pity we couldn't hear more of them. And now . . .

JANE: Can I . . . can I change places, I can't really . . . I mean I can't concentrate here . . . because of the lights up there, and him up there. (*She looks upwards at* REX*'s box.*)

LEONARD (*fast*): Jane's asked to change places, we'll allow that, but what we'll do is – I'll ask you a question and then you both have to change places, run round the table, and the first one there, will have their microphone switched on, and will be able to try to answer. (*He looks at* NICOLA; *smiles.*) Ready to run, girls! And the question is – what were the names of the four Beatles. Ready – steady – GO! (*They rush round the table, the long way. As they do so.*) The girls are running now – running round . . . and it's Jane who's there first, Jane who gets there. Now the Beatles.

JANE (*she struggles*): Paul McCartney, John . . . John . . .

LEONARD: Have to give their surnames too . . .

JANE: John . . . and Ringo . . . John . . .

LEONARD: Have to hurry you.

JANE: I can't . . . sorry.

LEONARD: You must know the names of the Beatles. (*He smiles.*) Now Nicola Davies, it's your big chance.

NICOLA: John . . . and Ringo . . . I can't remember the other one. (*She looks at him. Deliberate.*) I don't know the other name.

Very loud 'Don't know' noise.

LEONARD: Nicola's lost another life because of that. George Harrison, of course, was the answer. Nicola's only got one more life to her. Nothing to worry about. Now quick round we go again, we'll run before the question. Now! And they're off again, it doesn't take them long, panting and (*Loud.*) – round they go. (JANE *rushes round, but* NICOLA *walks it, not trying at all.* JANE *easily gets there first.*) That was about equal that time, I think – so we'll move on to the next question. (*He looks at* NICOLA.) To the final question of the Competition of the Century. And the great question is . . . (*Pause.*) Wait for it, who can do the loudest scream for Ross and the boys? Who can do the very loudest scream? Right now, watch the windows, Rex! And you at home, watch your radio, because they may break your sets, in fact they probably *will break* them. And shatter all your ornaments. Nicola Davies is first. You do a scream for us now, Nicola. (*Silence.*) Come on Nicola, do a scream. That's all you have to do. (*Funny voice.*) I'm sure she can do it. (NICOLA *sits still. Silence.*) Come on Nicola. (*'Competition' voice.*) You can do that, can't you, used to doing that. (NICOLA *looks up, opens her mouth slightly, swallows hard; no noise.*) You can scream for the boys, can't you. A really loud one. That's why you're here isn't it? (*Louder.*) Isn't it! You haven't got long, Nicola. (NICOLA *looks up, lets out a half-hearted scream.*) There! She's done it! That wasn't a very loud one, but now let's see what Jane can do. Ready Jane, just a scream for them.

JANE *sits up straight, lets out a very loud scream* –

*which starts loud, gets louder and louder and very very
long.*

LEONARD: Jane wins that. Jane wins that point. That is the
end of the Competition of the Century, and what is THE
SCORE?

REX (*calls*): Very close, Leonard, very close indeed.

LEONARD: The scores are very close, so we are in fact going
to invite you to cast your votes for the winner of our
prize, going off with the Boys, to the centre of the
universe, London Town. So ring us, on 55304, 55304, as
quick as *you* can, as from NOW. Just say 'Jane' or
'Nicola', that's all we require, if it's engaged, just dial
again at once. And hurry, we're waiting, high up here, in
our little box; put us out of our misery.

REX (*shouts*): He's here. Ross has arrived!

LEONARD: And we've just heard, Ross is here, in the
building, we've just felt the tremor go through it, and so,
while we wait, butterflies swarming in our stomachs, let's
have some proper music, a snatch of Rossini's 'Thieving
Magpie', followed by a razor-sharp commercial or two.
(*He puts on the music. They sit as it plays loudly. A long
pause. Total stillness. To the* GIRLS.) You can get down
now girls, if you want. (*He calls.*) Rex – get the girls a
cup of tea. (*He looks at them.*) Do you want a cup of tea?

JANE *nods.* MICK *enters, grinning happily.*

NICOLA (*quiet*): No thanks.

LEONARD (*his manner suddenly very quiet, withdrawn; to*
REX): Get Jane a cup of tea. And Nicola a glass of milk.
You must have something, Nicola. And also wipe the
spit off the mikes. (*He runs his hand along the desk.*)
And wipe this too, it's filthy.

81

REX (*coming down from box*): Len – that was . . . that was incredible.

LEONARD (*fast*): Was it? I can do without your comments.

MICK: Yes it was, Mr Brazil – really great.

REX: Yes it was. It really was? It was a knockout. (*Smiles.*) I've got Carol and everybody standing by. Everything's waiting.

> BIG JOHN *enters*.

LEONARD (*turns*): What are you doing there?

JOHN: Tremendous, Leonard. (*To* REX.) Wasn't it? (*He looks at the* GIRLS.) You OK, girls – bearing up? I've got some News for you now.

LEONARD (*turns*): I wasn't expecting the News, I thought it had moved.

JOHN (*smiling, unaware*): No, same schedule as always. Of course – (*Smiles.*) – life must go on.

> *Off-stage, one telephone bell starts ringing faintly; it's answered.*

REX: There we go. That's the first, they've started!

LEONARD: Get their drinks, Rex.

REX *goes*.

LEONARD: All right, girls, keep still where you are. Everyone keep still and don't speak. (*He moves to the mike, stops the records.*) And to interrupt there! For believe it or not, Big John is here with the local, national and international news.

> BIG JOHN *sits, begins to read the News, at first mundane items*.

LEONARD (*from the back wall in his strong DJ voice*): They call this News. (*He looks at* NICOLA.) Waste of time, isn't it. (BIG JOHN *is still reading. Louder.*) Do they call this news?

The telephone bells are growing louder, more numerous. BIG JOHN *starts reading more violent items. Suddenly* LEONARD *moves over to the table, presses a button, music bursts out.*

LEONARD (*'Competition' voice*): This is the Final here. Thank you, Big John, for reading the news for us. Now keep ringing . . . Keep those bells going ting-a-ling-a-ling, ring us, *please*. And while I wait, I'll spin another circle of happiness and pour a little more sugar over the city.

Music continues.

JOHN (*astonished*): I was only half-way through, Leonard.
LEONARD: That was enough News, wasn't it? I haven't spent a whole week whipping up the audience to lose them – let them drift away because of this. (*He picks up the news bulletin.*) It can wait an hour, can't it. (*Loud.*) It's going to, anyway.
JOHN (*picking up the bulletin*): All right then – if that's what you want. (*Smiles.*) If *you* say so, first time that's ever happened. But since it's all going so tremendously – (*Smiles.*) – you can't let much get in your way right this moment, I can see that. Certainly I've never heard you in better form. Never. (*He smiles again.*) Are you going to make a lot out of the announcement of the result then . . . ?

LEONARD (*sharp*): All right John.

REX enters with the drinks.

JOHN (*smiles*): He's given me the chop, the News has got

the chop for the first time.

REX: Yes, I heard – (*He gives drinks to the* GIRLS.)

JANE: Thank you. (*She tries to drink; it's very hot.*)

JOHN: But worth it just this once I think.

LEONARD (*not unpleasant*): Look, get out of here, John, go on – (JOHN *goes.*)

REX: Very soon now, girls, it'll be all over won't it? Leonard.

LEONARD (*back to him*): Yes?

REX: I wondered – I wondered if . . . *my minute* . . .

LEONARD: Did you? (*He cuts the music.*) Hello again – this is the control room, Competition Week – Leicester, England. Jane and Nicola are a little tense, aren't they, a little pale, but they're smiling bravely. Jane's rose is drooping slightly, Nicola's is bulging –

REX: Leonard . . . my minute . . .

LEONARD: Young Rex is here – calling out to me – he's very eager to have a chance to speak to you. Come here. (*He pulls* REX *forward.*) Here's your chance now, young Rex, how's it going?

REX: Hello – it's cracking along, Leonard, cracking. It's a great contest, isn't it, it's a fabulous contest, we're all agog back there – agog.

LEONARD: Are we. (*Staring at him.*) I see, Rex.

REX (*his voice getting louder, more confident*): The voting's very very close – the phones are jumping and ringing back there –

LEONARD: Jumping and ringing?

REX: Yes, Leonard – like they've got toothache. Want to hear it, folks? Want to hear them ringing folks? (*He bends the mike towards the bells.*)

LEONARD: We're not that posh anymore, are we – ?

REX: No – this is *my* voice now Leonard – this is a Rex-type voice. And I just want to say 'Hello' to the listening millions with it. (*Fast, smiling.*) We really seem to have stirred the whole population, Leonard, like soup, we had callers of all ages back there, all sorts, from nine to ninety, all kinds of voices. The machines are over-loading back there – it's terrifying, it's wonderful.

LEONARD: The machines are so busy back there, they're going to explode.

REX: That's right Leonard. Back there we really need six hands and six feet. (*Grins.*) And six tongues! The girls are looking very happy at the moment, waiting for the result, didn't they do well – put up a great show.

LEONARD: We're making the most of things, aren't we Rex – of our chances.

REX: That's right, Leonard – got to, haven't I. And it's a great feeling up here, a whale of a time – except the tension is killing me – stop the tension Leonard – please . . . stop it, don't leave me, Len, don't leave me! You must stop the tension, it's killing me, my left foot's already gone dead.

LEONARD: You're a bit of a joker, aren't you, Rex. (*Louder.*) A bit of a joker.

REX: That's what we all are, Leonard. (*Imitating* LEONARD*'s voice.*) That's why we're here folks – sitting up here, that's how we've been made, Leonard, isn't that right.

LEONARD: A bit of an aper, aren't we, Rex?

REX: That's what I am, Leonard.

LEONARD (*smiles*): And no questions asked.

REX: Of course not. No questions! That's all I can do, isn't it. I can't be any different. Play it again, Leonard.

LEONARD (*staring at him*): Play it again Rex. Rex likes the sound of his own voice, doesn't he?

REX: Yes! (*He laughs, standing over the mike.*) I like the

sound of my own voice all right. And I'd just like to say to the listening millions, it's intoxicating up here, folks. I'm flying with it, really flying. (*He looks at* LEONARD.) That's what we enjoy, folks, isn't it! No need to fear, Len and Rex are here. (*Sudden change of tone. Exuberant, brilliant.*) And look . . . look at this Leonard – see what's happening – I'm losing a little weight, Leonard, see it's slipping off, it's starting to slip off, getting more now – see, reels and reels of fat are dropping off me onto the floor, they are! That's right, at this very moment, I wish you could see it folks, Rex is losing the fat, it's just fallen off, whole streams of it coming away all over the studio, some's even gone over the controls, look at it Leonard, have you ever seen anything like it – have you – But seriously folks –

LEONARD: All right. That's enough, isn't it? (*He pulls him away from the mike.*) His hand is still gripping the microphone, he has to be torn away. Go and silence those bells – Rex, the girls can't wait any more.

REX (*smiling broadly*): I'll go and silence them right away. (*He calls into the mike.*) Last calls please! (*He goes.*)

LEONARD (*into the mike*): Rex has gone for the result . . . has even dressed like me today, folks. Don't worry, girls, we're there now!

NICOLA: Where do you want me to sit?

LEONARD: Sit here please, Nicola Davies. The girls are sitting by me now, I'm holding their hands, one each. They're sitting very straight very calm. 'They're tough girls you've got there, Brazil, they can take it!' Rex is bringing in the result – smiling proudly; that's a big envelope you're holding, Sound Engineer Rex.

REX: Yes, it is . . . Leonard.

LEONARD (*his tone is very quiet*): It has the word 'Winner' on the front in red ink. I'm opening the envelope, this is the moment we've hoped for – (*He looks at the card.*) And the words on the card are – (*He glances at* NICOLA.) – Jane Harris. (*Booming voice, repeating like a machine, fast.*) Jane Harris is the winner, Jane Harris is the winner, Jane Harris is the winner. Let's have some applause. (*He brings up tumultuous applause on tape.*) How do you feel, Jane? (*Applause dies away.*)

JANE (*very quiet*): I feel . . . I feel . . . I feel . . . OK . . .

LEONARD: You must be very happy.

JANE (*quiet*): I am, yes.

LEONARD: How does Nicola feel? No hard feelings, I hope?

NICOLA (*quiet*): I'm OK.

LEONARD: Sound Engineer Rex is now going to take you, Jane to where Ross is waiting. OK Rex, take her away.

REX: What? You mean me?

LEONARD (*not looking at him, with papers on desk*): Yes, you.

REX (*quietly, watching him*): You're not really letting me handle it all, are you?

LEONARD (*matter-of-fact*): Yes. It's what you want, isn't it?

REX: What? You're going to let me take her up – her up there and deal with Ross and all that?

LEONARD (*not looking up*): That's right. Go on.

REX (*suddenly loud*): Christ – that's incredible. That's really incredible! (*He takes* JANE*'s hand, pulls her towards the door.*) Come on, you're coming with me. (*He stops by the door.*) That's fantastic of you, Leonard. I'm not fired then.

LEONARD (*matter-of-fact*): No it doesn't seem you are. There's no stopping you, anyway.

REX (*looking at him*): I suppose not. (*Slight smile.*) Not now.

LEONARD (*not looking up*): Go on, get out of my sight.

REX (*smile*): Right, Leonard. (*He waits for a moment, then goes out with* JANE.)

> *Music in the background, allowing* LEONARD *to speak when he wants to.*

LEONARD: Rex . . . an unimagintive kid, isn't he . . . but going places! (LEONARD *glances up at* MICK, *who hastily leaves.* LEONARD *glances towards* NICOLA.) We'll be getting you a car, I hope, to run you back home. (*He is still pent up, brings music up slightly, switches onto air, red lights on, sings along to the record. DJ voice, very quiet, very tense.*) Any moment we'll be switching to Studio A, so wherever you are, whatever you're doing, *don't* go anywhere near the switch-off knob, because any minute now you'll be hearing the voice of Rex spreading out towards you – and just a reminder, the great group are going to Nottingham and Manchester, next Wednesday and next Saturday. (*He brings up the music.* NICOLA *touches the red lightbulb;* LEONARD *continues looking towards her.*) Don't touch that, it's hot.

NICOLA: Yeah – it is. (*She takes her hand away, picks up her glass of milk.*)

LEONARD (*red light on again*): I, Leonard Brazil, am taking a break now, a quick *snap*, a brrrreak. (*Calling.*) Come in, Studio A, come in there. Hello – come in Rex with the furry voice, it's all yours then!

REX'S VOICE (*on the intercom, booming over the loud-speakers*): Thank you Leonard for that introduction – Rex with the furry voice – there, we all liked that! And I have with me Jane, the lucky winner of the Competition of the Century, and the voice you've all been waiting for, in fact he's sitting in front of me and Jane right now, not only his voice, but *all of him*, the whole of the one and only, the greatest –

LEONARD *clicks it off.*

LEONARD: There.

NICOLA: Yes. (*Silence.*)

LEONARD *gets up, crumples a piece of paper.*

LEONARD: You OK?

NICOLA: Yes. (*She drops the full glass of milk; she hasn't drunk any of it.*)

LEONARD: Don't worry about that – it's a horrible mess in here anyway, isn't it?

NICOLA (*stares round the studio*): Yes.

LEONARD (*beginning to put on his jacket, and get his papers together*): Disgusting leftovers everywhere – the junk that's been sent in here, been pouring in, crammed away in every corner and going bad, probably; it's a nasty room, this, isn't it? (*He rubs the milk on the floor with his foot.*) This milk'll go grey-blue in a moment, hasn't been cleaned for months in here. (*Loud.*) It doesn't *look like* the nerve-centre of something does it? Are you all right? (*He stands ready to go; looks at her.*)

NICOLA: Yes, I'm OK.

LEONARD: Don't worry! We probably couldn't have let you win anyway – could we. Because you won that LP. It wouldn't have looked very good if you'd won both, would it. Might have smelt, as they say. (*Pause.*) So you couldn't really have won.

NICOLA (*quiet, blank*): No . . . I know.

LEONARD: And you've done all right, haven't you, fought your way up into here for the final. You've been quite lucky really . . . (*Pause. Louder as* NICOLA *doesn't react*.) You have, you know.

NICOLA: I know that, yes.

LEONARD: Good. Not much to see in London anyway. You mustn't believe what I've been saying about it, it's dead. (*Pause*.) She's not going in *their* car anyway, she's going in the second car of the convoy with the cook and the luggage. Half an hour's chat at midnight with them in a motorway cafe and that's all she'll get. (*Pause*.) Here – (*He picks up a tape*.) – there's the tape of Ross, we've been playing, you can have it, if you want. (*Then quick change*.) No, I think it's got to be returned, *they* want to use it again. Stop us cutting him up. (*Suddenly loud, changing tone, straight to her*.) You can't really like this shit, can you, do you really, deep down inside, like this music?

She doesn't reply.

LEONARD: Do you!

NICOLA: A bit.

LEONARD: A bit – what does that mean? Either you do or you don't.

NICOLA: Yes, I do.

LEONARD: Right! (*Pause*.) You know, Nicola, if, ten years ago, five years ago even – (*Mock voice*.) – when things were very different, I'd been told that I'd be doing this job, playing this mindless milk chocolate pap or manufactured synthetic violence endlessly to kids like you, I wouldn't have thought it remotely possible. (*Loud*.) Not at all, it's not exactly what I imagined happening, not even in my greyest moments. It's extraordinary really that things have resulted in *you*! Do you know that?

NICOLA *is in front of him, silent.*

90

LEONARD: I've been offered a job, too, Nicola, to do some more, a much much bigger job, to chatter and gibber to many more people, lots of them, all waiting for it. And they want a decision. Quick answer.

    NICOLA *watches him; he stares straight at her.*

LEONARD: This competition has been a great puller, you'll be pleased to know – the most successful of all, you're the only lucrative corner of the market left, that never fails, do you know that –

NICOLA (*staring straight at him*): Yes.

LEONARD: All you have to do is just stop buying, don't you, as simple as that, just stop, refuse to lap it up any more. Spit it out. *I mean that.* (*Suddenly loud.*) Do you – understand a word I'm saying?

NICOLA: Yes . . . I do.

LEONARD: I don't often meet any of my audience this close. I picked you out, do you know that, homed in on you . . . I picked out that voice, that slightly dead, empty sort of voice. Picked it out as Miss Average – which in fact you probably are not, and I followed that flat voice, each announcement was aimed at it.

NICOLA: Oh I see –

LEONARD: I let it get through each stage, let you clamber up here, because I wanted to see it . . . *meet you*, face you. (*Loud.*) And now you're here.

NICOLA (*quiet*): Yes.

LEONARD (*louder*): Is monosyllables all I'm going to get?

NICOLA: Yes.

LEONARD: What did you think of the Competition, then? (*Pause.*) Come on . . .

NICOLA: I don't know. (*She looks straight at him, cold.*) I don't know what I thought of it . . .

91

LEONARD (*abrasive*): Got a little out of hand – though it'll have sounded all right down there. Is that how you'd put it?

NICOLA: I don't know.

LEONARD: There was a touch of revenge, don't you think . . . I must want a little revenge . . . I glanced at you before the first question and saw that stare, that blank, infuriatingly vacant gaze, and then it just happened. I wanted to see just how far I *could push you*, how much you'd take – I was hoping you'd come back – that something would come shooting back, that you'd put up a fight Nicola. That you'd explode Nicola, you'd explode. Do you see, why didn't,why don't you . . . ? (*Suddenly very loud.*) What's the matter with all you kids now, what is it? Come on, answer me, you know what I'm talking about, you're not a small child, you know what I mean. (*Pause. Abrasive.*) Are you going to talk to me?

NICOLA: No.

LEONARD: Why not?

NICOLA: I . . . (*Slight pause.*) I don't want to.

LEONARD: You don't want to. (*Pause.*) Come here. (*Loud.*) You're not hoping to get away with that, are you? Come here – come on Nicola. (*He pulls her to him, holds her by the arm.*) There – After all, I brought you up here for this meeting – (*He stares down at her – slight smile.*) What are you going to do now, Nicola? (*Pause. She doesn't move.*) You don't even look startled! Nothing!

NICOLA: No.

LEONARD (*really loud*): COME ON! (*He takes hold of her and shakes her really violently for several seconds.*)

After a pause.

LEONARD: Had no effect on you at all.

NICOLA (*slightly louder*): No.

LEONARD (*still holding her*): You almost feel, Nicola Davies – as if you're from another planet, do you know that?

No answer. He turns.

LEONARD: I would give you a lift, love, but I'm going for a walk. Got to work things out. (*Very matter-of-fact.*) What are we going to do, *love*. (*She looks about her.*) Are you all right? (*He looks about the studio.*) You won't do anything silly – will you? No. (*He flicks on the switch:* ROSS's *voice booms out.*) There! (*He goes.*)

ROSS'S VOICE (*on the speakers*): The receptions we've been getting have been fabulous, *really* fabulous. You know, really warm, and we've had no bother, no trouble of any kind, everything's been calm and nice . . .

NICOLA *picks up her bag.*

ROSS'S VOICE: . . . which should put a sock in all those critics who've written about us. And to see those faces in the front row, they're always a special sort of face in the front row. I don't know how to describe it, but in the front row the faces are always different.

NICOLA *fastens her bag, moves out of the studio.*

REX'S VOICE (*on the speakers*): I know what you mean. I've noticed that myself.

NICOLA *moves into the shop area.*

ROSS'S VOICE (*on the speakers*): And also English front rows are very different, totally different in a funny kind of way from American front rows.

ROSS's *voice fades into the noise of the loud hum*

from the shop's fridge, as the lights go down on the studio and up on SUSAN *in the supermarket . . .*

Scene Three

The supermarket. NICOLA *stands facing* SUSAN, *who is standing opposite her holding a dustpan and brush. The shop has closed its doors for the evening. Silent and dark except for the light shining up from inside the fridge.*

SUSAN (*standing by the fridge*): Why are you so late? . . . I wondered if you'd show up at all.

NICOLA: I got delayed.

SUSAN: I've been hanging around for a long time. Everybody's gone, almost. Had to do this corner all by myself, and there was lots of it, bloody place. Done most of it now anyway. So you lost, didn't you.

NICOLA: Yes . . . that's right . . . I lost. (*Pause.* NICOLA *smiles slightly.*) You're right. (*She turns, bites her lip. Her mood is of contained violence.*)

SUSAN: You OK?

NICOLA: Yes, I'm OK. (*Louder.*) I'm all right. (*Pause.*) Did you hear it?

SUSAN: Yes, some of it.

NICOLA (*suddenly loud*): What do you mean, *some* of it?

SUSAN (*surprised*): No, I heard it. Quite a lot.

NICOLA (*very loud, savage*): Why didn't you hear all of it? (*Shouts.*) YOU SHOULD HAVE HEARD IT ALL! ALL OF IT! (*Pause, suddenly matter-of-fact.*) You'd only have been able to tell if you'd seen it. Been there. (*Pause.*) What did you think?

SUSAN: You were OK.

NICOLA (*pulls a fish-finger packet out of the fridge, lets it drop*): OK?

SUSAN: Ought to have won, really.

NICOLA: Yes, I know. (*Pause.*) It was very hot up there.

SUSAN: They really put you through it.

NICOLA: Yeah – they did. (*Sudden smile.*) Hey, look at that. (*She pulls a leg of the dummy out of her bag.*) It fell off! That's what they made me make . . .

SUSAN: That's right. (*Smiles.*) Should do it to it all.

> NICOLA *drops the bag with the dummy in it into the fridge. She smiles.*

NICOLA: Could put it in here, watch it go hard, freeze it, then pull it to bits easily. (*She pulls out the bag, stares into the fridge.*) Not much left in there, is there. (*Suddenly louder.*) Not much left!

SUSAN: Yes. (*She is bewildered by* NICOLA*'s aggression.*)

NICOLA (*fast*): It was interesting really seeing him, seeing the DJ there, that was interesting! (*Suddenly louder, quite clenched.*) It was all interesting – *everything*. (*She pulls more packets of fish fingers out of the fridge.*) Lot of these left, anyway.

> *As they talk,* NICOLA *keeps pulling more packets out, undoing packets and dropping them.*

SUSAN: You going to queue for the concert?

NICOLA: Don't think so. I don't want to. They're all right, I s'pose. But I'm not going this time.

SUSAN: I might go. I don't know.

NICOLA: We're too late – *because of this*. Never get a good place in the queue. We'd never get in.

SUSAN (*suddenly relaxing*): No we wouldn't, would we.

NICOLA: Anyway it's not worth it. It really isn't!

She is holding the bag very tight, with the dummy inside; clenched violence inside her.

SUSAN: Are you *all right*, Nicola? Not ill or anything?

NICOLA (*louder*): Yuh, I'm fine. I told you. There's nothing wrong with me. (*She glances behind her.*) It's all different here when it's dark. (*By the fridge again.*) Nobody's watching. We could throw all this out if we wanted. And all the rest, spread all over the shop – first thing they'd see Monday morning. They'd never know who it was.

SUSAN (*excited, uninhibited violence*): We can do the whole place, if we wanted, the cameras are off, dead, it wouldn't take long. The shelves come down easily, just fall off, and the stacks of cans, just have to pull one and millions come down, all pouring down. Could make them all do that. We could finish the whole place. It would be very easy really . . .

NICOLA: Yes. (*Loud.*) TEAR THROUGH IT IF WE WANTED. (*Pause.*) But it's not worth it really. I don't think it's worth it. Maybe next time. We'll see next time. (*Savage.*) I'll see next time.

SUSAN: What do you mean, next time?

NICOLA (*biting her lip*): I don't know, I don't know, do I?

SUSAN: You're in a funny mood, aren't you?

NICOLA (*clenched*): Yeah, that's right. I s'pose I am.

SUSAN: You are – never seen you like this –

NICOLA: No, that's right.

We hear the distant noise of a radio voice.

SUSAN: Sssh – hear that – listen to that.

NICOLA: What?

SUSAN: There – hear it now? That talking, that voice –

NICOLA: Yes.

SUSAN: Where's it coming from – somewhere near – very near. Can't see.

NICOLA: Don't know – but it's him all right.

The girls freeze. The lights go down on the supermarket and cross fade to the studio . . .

Scene Four

The studio. LEONARD *is standing over controls. He stops his own noise.*

LEONARD (*his tone is quiet, sharp, he takes the speed slowly*): Hello. That was of course LB's jingle, and this is a very special moment, for which I'm standing, I really am, all alone in this studio, standing above the controls, which are hot and steaming. Thank you to Rex for his first great solo over the air. Very smooth, very good. That was a Rex-type interview. (*His tone changes.*) I've got to tell you something now which is quite a big surprise, because today I was offered a very big job in London, with the very splendid Capital Radio – and they offered me a lot of money and a large, large audience, in London, the capital of this fine country of ours, and a fat programme, to do my very own thing. They offered me this job earlier today. 'We must have you,' they said. 'We must have him.' And I have thought about it. (*He smiles; loud, jubilant.*) And I have accepted their offer! Yes I have. I'm going there. I, Len Brazil, Lennnnnn Brazil, am leaving you for Capital Land, London! I hear it'll need four people to fill my job here, which is nice, but I'm going to London where all the action is – where I'll be giving a few jokes and all the hits and more, all the sounds and more, all the luck and more, where I'll be seeing us through our present troubles, obliterating the bad times – that's a Big Word – and remembering the good times, oh yes – and letting people remember and letting them forget. Drowning all our sorrows, yes I said drowning, till we're emerging out of the clouds, of course. And now I hope my voice is reaching out, spreading to the four corners of our area – across the whole city, through the blackness, swooping into cars on the motorway and down chimneys, and through brick walls and across pylons. (*His DJ voice.*) Over the whole domain, until it reaches you. Because I want to say, I'm sorry folks, but there it is. I'm sorry to leave you folks; but it's how I've always wanted to do things of course. (*Smiles to himself.*) What I wanted! Don't spit on the animals. I'm speaking to *you* now, I am, remember this, when you're in London, don't forget to give us a ring, want to hear from you, over the air, at the very least don't forget to tune in. Yes tune in! What are you doing Brazil – tell us – what on earth is he doing – He's saying *Goodbye* and *don't forget*. We're going to lick it, of course we will. No need to worry, no need to be sad. Shout that out. So tune in, I said tune in. Because I'll take your mind off things, oh yes. I will. (*He brings the music in louder.*) Hear that – some music! Music for Len's farewell. Tune in, I said. (*Very loud.*) TUNE IN. This is how we like it. I've got some great times for you, oh yes. You know I'll never let you down. That was Competition week. This is Len Brazil. Be seeing you.

Fade.

ACTIVITIES AND EXPLORATIONS

A   Keeping Track

The questions in this section are designed to help your reading and understanding of the play in the areas of plot, structure, character and interaction. They may be used as you read the play or afterwards, for discussion or for writing. Some are developed and expanded in the **Explorations** section.

Act One, Scene One

1   What day of the week is it?
2   What type of programme is Leonard broadcasting?
3   What is Leonard's attitude when he is 'on air'?
4   What is Leonard's attitude when he is 'off air'?
5   What is Rex's job?
6   What do we learn of Leonard's past?
7   'By the way, I've got Capital on the line.' Who are Capital and what is their interest in Leonard?
8   How does Leonard treat Rex?
9   Who are the Yellow Jacks? And why is Johnson (the station manager) insisting on 'maximum exposure' for their LP?
10   How does Leonard treat Angela and Rita, the phone-in contestants?
11   Why is Leonard 'suddenly interested' in Nicola Davies's voice?

Act One, Scene Two

1   In a performance, what would happen during the blackout?

2   What day of the week is it?

3   Lipton's is a chain of supermarkets: what are Nicola's and Susan's jobs there?

4   'I don't want trouble today, Susan.' What does Nicola's comment tell us about Susan?

5   What was it that happened to Susan that was so 'exciting'?

6   Why is Nicola so desperate to enter the competition?

7   Who is the 'you' to whom Leonard addresses himself while 'on air'?

Act One, Scene Three

1   What day of the week is it?

2   What is Mick's job? What does his attitude reveal of Leonard's status at Leicester Sound?

3   What does Rex do when he first enters? Why?

4   Why does Rex make Leonard 'feel nervous'?

5   What is John's job?

6   Why does Leonard try to put John off his job?

7   What is Leonard's reaction to the competition bribes?

8   Why does Leonard pay so much attention to the photographs?

9   Explain Leonard's reaction to Rex's story about the girl who had her lip autographed.

10   When does Leonard decide on Stage Two of the competition? Why does he laugh when he announces it on air?

11   Leonard says 'I don't like competitions'. Does he or doesn't he?

Act One, Scene Four

1   What day of the week is it?

2 How should Nicola's room be decorated and furnished?
3 What is Leonard's attitude to his listeners in this scene?
4 What is the attraction for Susan of doing anything she wants to the model of Ross?
5 Why does Susan tell the story about hitch-hiking?
6 What should Nicola be doing throughout this scene?
7 '*They strip the room*'. What is the significance of this stage direction? How should they do so?

Act One, Scene Five

1 What would take place during the blackout in performance?
2 What day of the week is it?
3 What is Leonard's attitude to hosting the phone-in?
4 Why is Rex working that night?
5 What are the tapes that Leonard shows to Rex?
6 Leonard says that he can 'Remember before the rot set in'. What does he mean?
7 What is **a)** Leonard's, and **b)** Rex's response to the models?
8 How does Leonard judge the models?
9 'I picked her voice out, that's all. I've been using it.' What has Leonard been using Nicola's voice for?
10 Why does Rex get fired?
11 What is the 'LB Spot'?
12 What comes over Leonard during the 'LB Spot'? And what is Rex's reaction?

Act Two, Scene One

1 What day of the week is it?
2 What is Nicola doing at the start of the scene?

101

3 What is Susan's mood?

4 Why is Leonard telephoning Nicola again?

5 How does Nicola feel about her visit to Leicester Sound?

6 Why does Susan force-feed Nicola?

Act Two, Scene Two

1 What is Leonard's attitude to the offer of the job at Capital?

2 What did John do before he worked at Leicester Sound and how did he get the job there?

3 Why does Leonard threaten Rex again?

4 What is Leonard's reaction to Nicola when he meets her?

5 How does Leonard treat Jane on her arrival?

6 What differences are there between what happens in the studio and what gets broadcast during the competition?

7 How does the atmosphere in the studio change during the word game?

8 Do the words selected by Leonard in the word game have any significance?

9 What does Jane's speech tell us about her character?

10 Why does Leonard help Nicola during her speech?

11 Why does Nicola stop trying during the race section?

12 How does Leonard's attitude change after the competition?

13 What is the station staff's reaction to the competition?

14 Why does Leonard interrupt the news?

15 What change has come over Rex on air? And what is Leonard's reaction to the 'new' Rex?

16 Do we know whose name is on the winner's card?

17 Why does Leonard give Rex the interview with Ross?

18 How did Leonard hope Nicola would react to the competition? Why?

19 How does Leonard attempt to provoke a reaction from Nicola now?

20 How does Nicola react?

Act Two, Scene Three

1 Why does Nicola empty out packets of fish fingers?

2 What does the stage direction '*clenched*' mean?

3 What is Susan's reaction to Nicola and the competition?

4 How should Nicola say her last line?

Act Two, Scene Four

1 Why is Leonard '*jubilant*'?

2 What does the speech reveal about Leonard's state of mind?

3 Why has Leonard decided to take the job with Capital?

4 'You know I'll never let you down.' Why does Leonard say this now?

Explorations

The questions in this section are more detailed and rely on your having read the whole play. Some of the questions develop ideas from the **Keeping Track** section: because these questions are more detailed they offer the opportunity to develop the ideas into written, oral or practical coursework assignments. Some will require a close knowledge of the play; others will require an imaginative response.

A Characters

Leonard Brazil

1 Account for the differences between Leonard on air and Leonard off air in Act One, Scene One. What do they reveal of his character?

2 How important is the fact that Leonard was a teacher before working for Leicester Sound? What similarities does his work as a disc-jockey have to his former work as a teacher?

3 'I do it to everyone that works for me.' Giving examples from the play, explain Leonard's attitudes to the people that work with and for him.

4 'Your mouth tastes bitter, Brazil' says Leonard during the 'LB Spot' at the end of Act One, Scene Five. What does Leonard have to be bitter about?

5 'Do you ever listen to your words Brazil? Never, thank goodness, but never mind.' Again, Leonard says these words during the 'LB Spot'. Does Leonard listen to his words on air? Does he mind?

6 What does Nicola Davies represent to Leonard? Why must he meet her?

7   What does Leonard hope to achieve in his meeting with Nicola? Is he successful?

8   'I don't like competitions'. Refer in detail to the play in explaining whether you think Leonard does or does not like competitions.

9   'London Town, where everything is still possible.' Why does Leonard finally accept the offer of the job with Capital at the moment of his greatest triumph at Leicester Sound?

10 Using the play as a whole, analyse Leonard's style as a disc-jockey. What is his relationship and his attitude to his audience on air?

11 What do Leonard's monologues at the end of each act reveal? Consider the character's state of mind at the time of the delivery of the monologue within the structure of the play.

12 In presenting the character of Leonard on stage, what aspects of his character would you highlight? How would you convey them successfully to an audience?

13 Write the script for the introduction of Leonard's first show for Capital. How will he introduce himself to his new audience?

14 Is Leonard Brazil a wholly believable creation? What does Stephen Poliakoff intend to do in stretching the limits of our belief?

Nicola Davies

1   Analyse and explain the effect Nicola has upon Leonard in Act One, Scene One.

2   What impression should the audience form of her in Act One, Scene One?

3   What does Nicola Davies represent to Leonard Brazil?

4   What does Nicola hope to achieve through entering the competition?

5   What do we learn of Nicola's work and home background?

6   What is the tone of Nicola's speech about the concert in Act Two, Scene Two? What does the speech reveal about her interests and expectations? What does it add to what we already know about the character?

7   How is Nicola affected by her visit to Leicester Sound?

8   If Nicola kept a diary, what would she write in it on the Saturday night after the competition?

9   In presenting the character of Nicola onstage, what aspects of her character would you highlight? How might you convey them successfully to an audience?

Rex

1   Explain the working and the personal relationship between Rex and Leonard in Act One.

2   What does Leonard represent to Rex?

3   What does Rex represent to Leonard?

4   How does the character of Rex change throughout the play? How might these changes be conveyed successfully by an actor to an audience?

5   What is the function of the character of Rex in the play?

Susan

1   What do we learn of Susan's character in Act One, Scene Two?

2   'Why don't you keep still?' says Nicola to Susan in Act Two, Scene One. Why doesn't she 'keep still'?

3   In presenting the character of Susan onstage, what aspects of her character would you highlight? How might you convey these successfully to an audience?

4 What is the function of the character of Susan in the play?

B Themes

1 What is the *City Sugar* of the title? What are its effects on the person who serves it and on the people who consume it?

2 Analyse Leonard's relationship with his listeners: how does he talk to, treat and keep his audience?

3 Leonard Brazil is the reason for Leicester Sound's success: from the evidence of the play, account for this success.

4 Why is Competition Week so important to Leicester Sound?

5 What effect does Leonard Brazil feel and fear he has upon his listening audience?

6 Leonard says he has been 'using' Nicola's voice. How else has he used her? What other examples of exploitation are presented in the play?

7 Leonard Brazil is presented as a successful broadcaster. Why, then, is he unable to communicate on a personal level with Nicola Davies?

8 What does Poliakoff want us to think about the people who listen to and enjoy Leonard Brazil's show?

9 The world of the play is never silent: what is the effect of this upon the characters who inhabit this world?

10 'Don't spit on the animals!' Who are the animals? How and why are they treated as such?

11 Script a phone-in competition between two contestants, with Leonard Brazil as the host, which has a pair of concert tickets as the prize. How will the competition be handled by Leonard? What questions will be asked? How will the contestants be treated?

12 What are Stephen Poliakoff's intentions in writing the play? How successfully has he realised those intentions?

C   In Performance

1 Draw up a design brief for the play as a whole. Consider the sets required, as well as the need to get from one to the next easily in performance, including the furniture and props needed. Consider also the costumes for the characters: how might they suggest character? Use evidence from the text to justify your decisions.

2 How should the 'Competition of the Century' be presented on stage? What should be the audience's reaction to it?

3 What is the style of the play? How might an audience react to what it sees developing onstage? Choose specific examples if you wish.

4 What reactions does Stephen Poliakoff intend the audience to have to the *content* of the play? How does he set about achieving them? Would he be successful in achieving the reactions he intends?

D   Criticism

1 Poliakoff's plays are 'centred on strong characters – often a dominant character who has a clearly defined or striking function in contemporary life' (John Russell Brown). What is Leonard Brazil's function? How does he achieve it?

2 'Poliakoff attacks a series of readily identifiable targets'. What are those targets in *City Sugar*? How successful are the attacks?

3 Ronald Hayman writes that Leonard's final speech brings his 'self-contempt into focus'. On what is Leonard's self-contempt founded?

4 'The dominant images tend to be those of alienation' (C.W.E. Bigsby). How successful is the alienation Poliakoff seeks to convey communicated through the play?

APPENDIX

Plays and Films of Stephen Poliakoff

Stage Plays

1969 *Granny*: Westminster School.
1971 *Day With My Sister*: Edinburgh.
1971 *Lay-By*: Royal Court Theatre, London
1972 *Pretty Boy*: Royal Court Theatre, London.
1974 *Sad Beat Up*: London.
1974 *The Carnation Gang*: Bush Theatre, London.
1974 *Clever Soldiers*: Hampstead Theatre, London.
1975 *Heroes*: Royal Court Theatre, London.
1975 *Hitting Town*: Bush Theatre, London.
1975 *City Sugar*: Bush Theatre, London.
1976 *City Sugar*: Comedy Theatre, London.
1977 *Strawberry Fields*: National Theatre, London.
1978 *The Summer Party*: Sheffield.
1978 *Shout Across the River*: London.
1979 *American Days*: London.
1981 *Favourite Nights*: London.
1984 *Breaking the Silence*: Royal Shakespeare Company, Barbican and West End, London.
1986 *Coming in to Land*: National Theatre, London.

Television

1978 *Stronger than the Sun*.
1980 *Bloody Kids*.
1980 *Caught on a Train*.
1982 *Soft Targets*.

Films

1984 Screenplay *Runners*.
1988 Screenplay and Directed *Hidden City*.

110

YELLOW BLUES
Slowly

WELL YOU KNOW THE BLUES THAT MAKE YOU SAD THE

BLUES THAT MAKE YOU BLUE IF YOU'RE FEEL-ING KIND-A BAD I'VE

bouncy

GOT THE BLUES FOR YOU SING THE YEL-LOW BLUES

SING THE YEL-LOW BLUES AND THE YEL-LOW BLUES

WILL MAKE YOU SMILE A – GAIN SING THE YEL-LOW BLUES

I CAN GIVE YOU LOVE
slow ballad – lilting beat

I'LL GIVE YOU AP-RIL SHOW-ERS   DAFF-O-DILS IN MA-
-Y   I'LL GIVE YOU JUNE-TIME FLOW-ERS   RO-SES EV-ERY DA-
-Y   DON'T YOU THINK THAT MA-Y-BE   YOU COULD BE MY
BA --- BY MY SWEET LIT-TLE ANG-EL FR'M A-- BUVE 'CAUSE I CAN GIVE YOU
LOVE*(YES! CAN) I CAN GIVE YOU LOVE*(BE YOUR MAN) BE MY LIT-TLE
BA - BY DON'T YOU THINK THAT MAY-BE I CAN GIVE YOU LOVE
I LOVED YOU IN DEC-EM-BER--- -

*(These lines are sung by another singer on the record at the
beginning of Act Two. but not by JANE in the competition.
She leaves a pause, and beats time nervously with her foot.)

THE HEREFORD PLAYS
General Editor: E. R. Wood

John Arden
*Serjeant Musgrave's
    Dance*

Alan Ayckbourn
Confusions

Peter Barnes
The Ruling Class

Robert Bolt
A Man for All Seasons

Bertolt Brecht
*The Caucasian Chalk
    Circle*

Chapman and Coxe
Billy Budd

Brian Clark
*Whose Life Is It
    Anyway?*

Shelagh Delaney
A Taste of Honey

Nikolai Gogol
The Government Inspector

Greenwood and Gow
Love on the Dole

Willis Hall
*The Long and the Short and
    the Tall*

Stanley Houghton
Hindle Wakes

Henrik Ibsen
An Enemy of the People

D. H. Lawrence
*The Widowing of Mrs
    Holroyd and The
    Daughter-in-Law*

Arthur Miller
*The Crucible
Death of a Salesman
All My Sons
A View From the Bridge*

Bill Naughton
Spring and Port Wine

André Obey
Noah

John Patrick
*The Teahouse of the August
    Moon*

Luigi Pirandello
*Six Characters in Search of
    an Author*

Stephen Poliakoff
City Sugar

J. B. Priestley
*An Inspector Calls
When We Are Married*

R. C. Sherriff
Journey's End

David Storey
In Celebration

J. M. Synge
*The Playboy of the Western
    World* and *Riders to the
    Sea*

John Whiting
A Penny for a Song

Oscar Wilde
*The Importance of Being
    Earnest*

Emlyn Williams
*The Corn is Green
Night Must Fall*

Tennessee Williams
*The Glass Menagerie
A Streetcar Named Desire*